Erich Schröder

Dear Earth, take Care!

Erich Schröder

Dear Earth, take Care!

A very personal reflection on the
current situation of people on earth,
inspired by news and discussions.
from print media, TV and books
from the year 2020 and the
first quarter of 2021.

9 783753 454986

Bibliographic Information of the German
Nationalbibliothek: The German National Library
lists this publication in the German National Bibliography;
detailed bibliographic data are available on the Internet at
http://dnb.dnb.de.

© 2021 Dr. Erich Schröder

Production and Publishing:
BoD – Books on Demand, Norderstedt

ISBN: 9 783753 454986

INHALT

Dear Earth,

first of all, I must compliment you: You are beautiful, really beautiful! I had the chance to see and experience much of you, and I was always overwhelmed by your diversity and beauty. Your landscapes, mountains, rivers, oceans, coasts, deserts, your vegetation, the diversity of forests, plants, flowers, the diversity of species in the animal world from elephants to ants, and finally your climate, which offers a comfort zone for people, animals, and plants like probably on no other star. Your uniqueness, which made our life on you possible in the first place.

Unfortunately, in the last hundred years - a second in your lifetime - we have not always behaved well towards you. Your seemingly eternal beauty has suffered, it has developed wrinkles that don't look good on you at all. Your oceans and now your beaches are full of plastic waste. Your beautiful rainforests are being cut down, burned, or poisoned by faulty oil wells. We have polluted your waters and damaged your atmosphere and climate with our exhaust fumes. For several decades now, we have suspected that our highly praised progress, consumption, and lifestyle are far beyond your resources and capacities. The realization is by no means new, we have just successfully suppressed it for a long time. In the meantime, the consequences of our way of life are already showing themselves even more seriously beyond the given conditions.

Even if the beauty of your landscapes and of the animal and plant world suffers heavily under our bad influence. You will survive it - we, however, may not. Stephen Hawking was probably the most prominent physicist of our time. He gave already in 2017, few years before his death, the prognosis that in 100 years the bases of life of humans on earth would be destroyed so far that mankind would die out. Only his conclusion to emigrate to a distant planet for the preservation of mankind, I cannot follow. A barren and inhospitable Martian landscape without atmosphere and viable climate is hardly a real substitute for you, our beautiful Earth, even if our technology would make a survival there perhaps possible.

Because you, dear Earth, are really an amazing entity with almost fantastic and for your living beings ideal characteristics. Despite your high age of about 4.5 billion years, there is still an almost inexhaustible glow inside you, a huge reservoir of energy. Occasionally, when a volcano erupts, we can see a small piece of your embers and sense your tremendous powers. Forces that in the course of time have piled up mountains and shifted entire continents as if in a puzzle. Equally immeasurable are your water resources, without which our life would not be possible, and which also decisively shape your climate. And finally, you have this comparatively thin layer of atmosphere, which makes life on land possible and in which your climate takes place. This combination of your properties is unique, each for itself and all together. To our knowledge so far, there is no comparable star in the universe with these properties in this combination.

Even more we should make every effort to protect, nurture and preserve you - not least to safeguard our own livelihoods. Most of us have understood this by now. Nevertheless, there are obviously some circumstances that make it exceedingly difficult to change our previous and still harmful behavior and to prevent further destruction of these bases of life. And although we would actually be intellectually and technically capable of doing so, it is by no means certain that we will succeed in making the necessary change in time. The gloomy prognosis of Stephen Hawking hovers over us.

Dear Earth, so let's take a sober look at the current situation.

Wonderful Modernity

"*We did not inherit the Earth from our parents - we borrowed it from our children.*" This phrase, often quoted by environmental activists, is sold as "ancient Indian wisdom," but its actual origin is rather unknown. The message of the wisdom is clear, a warning regarding the current climate and environmental problems that will ultimately burden following generations. The reference to this is an important appeal and a fitting image, but just one side of the coin. Because of course every generation inherits its living conditions, together with the condition of the earth, from the parents and passes all this on to its children sometime. We should not turn this into a conflict of generations, that would be about the last thing we need right now. Let's take a closer look at the current "handover of the earth". There is hardly any reason for a conflict because the bottom line is not so bad. Of course, every balance sheet has negative balances as well as positive ones.

Let's start with the positive balance. In almost every respect, the outgoing postwar generation leaves behind the best living conditions ever seen in Germany - and that built on the ruins of the Second World War. Probably the most important factor is a 75-year period of peace, unique in Germany and Europe. But almost everything else has developed for the better during this period. I will spare myself a list of the many improvements here and refer to the books of the Swiss journalist Guido Mingels ("Früher war alles schlechter," Deutsche Verlags-Anstalt), who writes in the preface of his first book (2017):

"Much speaks for the fact that man has never had it better on earth than just now, in the present. Health is improving. Life expectancy is increasing. Infant mortality is falling, almost everywhere in the world. Wealth is increasing, also almost everywhere. Birth rates are decreasing, as is maternal mortality. Poverty is decreasing; it has decreased more in the last 50 years than in the 500 years before that. Education is improving; four out of five people can now read and write. War deaths are decreasing, murder rates are falling. Vaccination rates are rising, diseases are disappearing. Agricultural yields per area multiplied. Forests are growing. Hunger is dwindling. Working hours are shrinking. There are fewer victims of natural disasters, fewer AIDS deaths, and fewer

working children. Germans drink less alcohol, smoke less and kill themselves less often. The list is long."

Even if there are a few points where things are going backwards again today (2021), for example regarding forests, the overall development is overwhelmingly positive. With 115 impressive examples, Guido Mingels meticulously shows in his two books what the improvements consist of in detail. And then there are also groundbreaking innovations that have changed the world, such as the Internet and the smartphone. A world without Google, Amazon, Facebook & Co.? Hard to imagine today! And who would want to do without the convenience of their smartphone today, e.g. making free calls to the whole world from anywhere at any time with some apps? I still remember well the time when a phone call to a friend in Peru cost DM 50 for the first three minutes. And more groundbreaking inventions are just around the corner: The chance of beating cancer in a few years, for example, is not bad.

And that brings us to the negative balance. Let's start right here with the Internet, which has now also revealed its many dark sides. It offers corresponding anonymous forums for communication and trade for everything imaginable that is bad: weapons, drugs, child pornography and much more. Computer viruses enable fraud, theft, sabotage, and blackmail on a large scale with damage that can hardly be measured. Platforms like Facebook, with billions of customers, use their algorithms to manipulate opinions on an enormous scale and, by abusing their structures, even to bring about political change, e.g., by manipulating elections.

Increasing prosperity and standard of living as well as mobility also have considerable side effects that are becoming more and more apparent and are now already having a profoundly serious impact: Climate change with all its consequences, overfishing of the oceans with their simultaneous massive littering especially by plastic waste and oil, as well as uncontrolled and thus conflict-ridden migration movements towards the affluent nations. These undesirable side effects of increasing prosperity have gone unnoticed or ignored for far too long.

The bottom line is that younger generations have been starting their lives as adult citizens for a good 50 years at an unprecedented and ever-increasing level of prosperity and quality of life. For this life, they have a choice of options and opportunities like no other generation before. At the same time, however, there are currently several severe problems that require short-term and sustainable solutions in order not to seriously endanger the stability of our living conditions on earth.

Let's get one thing straight right here: This is not an extraordinary burden on a younger generation. The post-war generation also had its severe problems at the beginning, the prevailing poverty, the cold war between East and West with an acute nuclear threat, and massive environmental pollution caused by a rapidly growing industry without protective measures. All of this has been resolved quite satisfactorily. Examples include arms control treaties and improvements in air quality in the Ruhr-district or water quality in the Rhine river. The generations before, during and between the world wars had to cope with even more massive and existential problems. (To be read in the authentic diaries of a family, published by Gerd Schröder in "Werth und Overhoff," Books on Demand, 2020)

I consider the current problems to be quite solvable intellectually and technically with a concerted effort. Why, despite all my confidence in our science and technology, I nevertheless have reservations as to whether mankind will succeed in finding the necessary short-term and sustainable solutions to the problems, we will discuss in the following chapters.

Corona is only the Beginning

The Corona pandemic has affected almost the entire world and disrupted its previous daily routine. Urgent other problems, such as climate change, unfortunately lost their focus as a result. The number of people who have died from Corona is in the millions, and many more have fallen ill or will fall ill. In many places, medical care for the sick is at its limit or already beyond it. The economic and social consequences of the pandemic are also enormous. Aviation, a major factor in the spread of the pandemic, has been marginalized in a noticeably short time and will not recover from this anytime soon - if ever it will take years. The previously thriving tourism industry is down. The cruise ships that have recently been so popular, albeit environmentally harmful, are bobbing around empty at sea in some cases because parking for the ships would be more expensive. What a gross nonsense! The entire gastronomy, hotels, and restaurants is struggling to survive, either had to close or has practically hardly any traveling guests. Theaters and cinemas have had to close, concerts and exhibitions have been canceled, the entire cultural scene has shut down, except for a few street musicians. Culture no longer takes place. Small businesses and individual entrepreneurs, like artists, have lost their last customers to cutbacks and austerity measures.

The state tries to alleviate the misery with various support payments, which unfortunately often reach those affected late. In addition, however, crooks also obtain these funds by fraud. All in all, the national debt is growing to gigantic proportions.

Citizens have been dreaming for a good year that everything will return to the way it was before the pandemic. But that may take some time, certainly until the end of 2021, perhaps even into next year. The pandemic and the measures to combat it have had a massive impact on people's daily lives. People are becoming restless, irritable, and many even aggressive under the considerable restrictions on daily life. As early as November 2020, everyone was talking about the need to have Christmas after all. The policy quickly buckled and allowed private Christmas parties with up to 10 people plus children - and the same for New Year's Eve and New Year. A Christmas party in a warm living room with three generations and more than 10 people, maybe also with singing Christmas carols together? Knowing full well that the virus spreads via aerosols in the air we breathe? Fortunately, in view of the sharp rise in the number of infections and deaths, politicians have finally issued somewhat stricter rules for the festive season. To what extent the population complied is another question. In any case, as expected, it was a "happy holiday" for the virus, and the number of infections rose sharply. A few weeks later, in January, more than 1,000 victims of the virus were counted every day - a high price for a pusillanimous policy that did not dare to impose the bitter reality, the necessary renunciation of the traditional Christmas meetings, on the people.

Then the first mutations of the virus were discovered, some of them even more contagious than the original version. Although in the meantime, after sensationally fast research and development processes, the first approved vaccines are available in limited quantities, the concern remains about a renewed flare-up of the pandemic in further and ever stronger waves. Will the vaccines also protect against these and other mutants of the virus? Even if they do, however, it will be another year or two before a significant portion of humanity is protected for the time being. It is likely that, as with the flu vaccine, annual boosters with protection against new mutants will be required.

But will things ever return to the way they were before the pandemic? And do we really want that? Or, after the severe shocks caused by the pandemic, is there not even a chance for a new beginning that avoids previous undesirable developments? Would there be a concept for this, a master plan?

A return to the past is, of course, in line with the current yearning of the majority. But that would probably only be an intermediate state. Because sooner or later, the restrictions caused by the pandemic will be followed by other and more far-reaching restrictions due to climate change. Or perhaps because of a mutation of the virus, or because of a new pandemic. In 2020, millions of minks had to be killed in Denmark because the animals were affected by the Corona virus. It shows that when humans and animals meet in animal husbandry, there is always a risk of transmission, host change and mutation of viruses. Animal viruses pass to humans and vice versa. The current coronavirus probably originated in bats; the animal intermediate host for transmission to humans is not yet known. It is probably an animal species sold in the animal market of Wuhan, China. This city is believed to be the origin of the pandemic. Similar transmissions are possible again at any time.

So back to cheap flights and Ballermann, to SUVs and "free driving" on the highway, to factory farming, excessive meat consumption and barracked harvest workers? Do we really want that? Or do we perhaps prefer to use the Corona shock for a period of reflection and a sustainable and environmentally conscious new beginning?

We have some time to think about it, because the pandemic, even if vaccinations have started now, will certainly be with us for at least the whole of 2021. Experts do not yet dare to make any reliable predictions about when the pandemic will finally be defeated. But we shouldn't allow ourselves too much time either; a concept for the future should be initiated before public life has settled back into its old tracks. Is there already a plan B? Unfortunately, it doesn't look that way; the longing for the former state is probably just too great. But the next pandemic is sure to come, as are the consequences of climate change, which are already becoming clear. After the terrible experiences of the Second World War, humanity came to its senses and came together to establish and launch some common initiatives, for example the United Nations, the World Health Organization, and the World Bank. Such initiatives are also needed now to address some urgent problems. We need to come together again!

The Power of Climate Change

The critical look at climate began around 1975, but climate change was more of a niche issue at that time. In February 1979, politicians, and scientists from 53 countries met for the first World Climate Conference in Geneva. It was decided to develop a world climate program and to establish an Intergovernmental Panel on Climate Change (IPCC). The IPCC is a scientific organization supported by 195 countries of the United Nations that compiles all relevant data on climate change and publishes them in regular reports. In 2007, the IPCC, together with former U.S. Vice President Al Gore, was awarded the Nobel Peace Prize for its efforts to raise global awareness of climate change. At that time, however, public awareness of the problem was only rudimentary. Today, on the other hand, climate change is generally regarded as the most serious threat to humanity due to the increasing warming of the atmosphere. The first effects of this threat are already clearly visible.

The cause of current climate events is shown by the so-called Keeling curve, a continuous measurement of carbon dioxide (CO_2) concentration at the Mauna Loa Observatory on Big Island, Hawaii. The curve shows a slightly progressive increase in CO_2 concentration of 100ppm over the last 60 years, from about 320 to 420ppm. That doesn't sound so dramatic, but it's more than will result from natural processes over 6,000 years during the transition from an ice age to a warm period, said Professor Gerald Haug, paleoclimatologist and president of the prestigious Leopoldina, in an interview (Der Spiegel, Oct. 27, 2020). Humanity, Haug said, "currently burns 10 billion tons of carbon every year in the form of oil, coal and gas, so it produces about 36 billion tons of CO_2." By far, China currently emits the most CO_2, followed by India; next in line are the U.S. and Europe.

Most scientists assume that there is a direct link between the climate changes currently observed and the CO_2 concentration in the atmosphere. They blame this on the so-called greenhouse effect. According to this theory, CO_2, like the glass of a greenhouse, impedes the escape of heat into space, the more concentrated the more effective. This is important to prevent the lower atmosphere from cooling down to the point of a new ice age. However, if the CO_2 concentration continues to increase, the lower atmosphere will continue to heat up due to solar radiation. Such a slow increase in temperature is being observed right now. This has dramatic consequences.

After all, climate change is already making itself clearly felt: Melting glaciers in the Alps, the Andes and many other mountains, the increase in hurricanes and forest fires and an increasing drought, also in Germany. The predictions of science have apparently not been exaggerated. According to a study by the University of Leeds, the Earth has "lost," i.e., converted to meltwater, about 28 trillion tons of ice within 23 years. The Arctic ice sheet lying on top of the water is just melting faster and faster. Since the ice is in the water anyway, this has no immediate effect on the level of sea level. However, the decreasing white ice layer reduces the reflection of sunlight, which then penetrates the darker water with its heat and thus accelerates the warming and melting even more, just as with the melting of glaciers in the mountains. If, on the other hand, the ice cover over Greenland were also to melt, sea level could rise by up to six meters. Sea levels are already rising today, by an average of 3 millimeters per year worldwide. On a linear projection, that would be 30 centimeters at the end of this century, compared with 17 centimeters in the past century. Some forecasts for this century, however, go far beyond this, up to 110 centimeters, because they do not consider a linear projection of the rise in temperatures to be realistic due to self-reinforcing processes in this development. The rise in sea level currently still varies greatly from region to region. The German coasts have so far been affected to a below-average extent, but this may change soon. However, the frequency of storm surges has increased significantly over the years. On the west coast of the Americas, by contrast, the level of the Pacific is rising about four times as fast as the global average.

Almost a quarter of the land surface of the Northern Hemisphere consists of permafrost, or ice and frozen earth. As the lower atmosphere warms, these soils are now beginning to thaw faster than expected. Over time, organic materials have decayed beneath the ice-tight surface, creating methane gas. Methane is considered to be 28 times more climate-changing than CO_2. If the frozen surface now thaws under warming, this methane gas is released and escapes into the atmosphere. It is estimated that up to 1,600 billion tons of carbon could be stored in the permafrost. A fatal self-reinforcing process looms: warming allows the methane to escape, which further accelerates atmospheric warming. That would be a point at which global warming can no longer be influenced by humans.

Some of the methane released is broken down by photochemical reactions in the atmosphere and by methanotrophic bacteria in the soil. These are found in the boundary layers of permafrost soils, but also especially in forest soils, where they do not find methane in the soil, but then take it from the atmosphere. Forest soils are thus particularly important for lowering methane concentrations in the air. Conversely, the loss of forest areas, e.g. in the Amazon region, is thus particularly critical with regard to climate change.

In addition to deforestation and arson, spontaneous forest fires also lead to the loss of forest areas, which are dramatically increasing in frequency and intensity in several regions of the world. Increasing atmospheric warming is a contributing factor, as are increasing regional droughts. The North American west coast, Australia and Siberia are particularly affected. In 2020, wildfires reached historic proportions in the western United States and in southeastern Australia. However, Germany also experiences forest fires every year, some of which are severe. The increasing dryness in some German regions leads to fears of bad things to come. The forest fires not only destroy the trees, which are so important as CO_2 reservoirs, but also release their stored CO_2, so that this additionally escapes into the atmosphere. In Siberia, not only forests but also peat soils are burning, which releases large amounts of CO_2. The fires also cause the permafrost there to thaw more deeply, which releases methane. Thus, CO_2 and methane together accelerate climate change through a disastrous cycle of mutual amplification.

Global warming also affects the Earth's water cycle. Warmer air can absorb more moisture, which makes rainfall and tropical cyclones more frequent and stronger. Already, such hurricanes are causing tremendous damage. In 2017, Hurricane Maria alone, the highest category 5, caused a total of an estimated US$94 billion in damage - and that was just days after Hurricane Irma, also category 5 and causing significant destruction, passed through. The annual number of these storms has roughly doubled since 1980. With global warming, precipitation is shifting in a trend that today's dry areas are becoming even drier, and today's rainy areas are receiving even more precipitation.

Agriculture, too, is particularly affected by climate change. Rising temperatures, drought and extreme weather threaten crop cultivation and animal husbandry. Previously stable crop cycles and yields are thrown out of balance. For Germany's agriculture, the increasing dryness of the soil is a particular challenge. But the changes are also eating away at crop yields worldwide and thus threatening the global food situation. Around 815 million people are currently going hungry worldwide. To ensure sufficient food for all, global agricultural production would have to increase by around 60 percent by 2050; the Intergovernmental Panel on Climate Change (IPCC), on the other hand, expects production to fall by 10 to 25 percent during this period. At the same time, agriculture accounts for around 10 percent of total climate gas emissions (CO_2, methane). Livestock farming is particularly important here, with cattle alone producing around 50 percent of methane emissions in Germany. Thus, the high consumption of meat in the western industrialized countries contributes significantly to the increase in CO_2 and methane. Nitrous oxide, which is produced during nitrogen fertilization, is also very harmful to the climate.

Farmers are trying to produce crops that are more resistant to the effects of climate change by means of new breeding and mutations. The interventions in genetic structures that are sometimes necessary for this are viewed critically because of possible unplanned effects. In the EU, the spread of genetically modified varieties has not yet been permitted. Other approaches from the UN World Food Program (WFP) are experimenting with large-scale hydroponics for growing vegetables in cities but also in infertile areas of the world.

In an experimental facility in Saxony-Anhalt, the Helmholtz Center for Environmental Research has been testing the influence of the climate changes still expected in this century on plants and animals for six years on an experimental area of about seven hectares. To do this, the researchers are simulating the temperature and humidity conditions as they would likely develop if the atmospheric temperature were to rise by an average of 2 degrees. The results so far are frightening on the one hand, but also show ways to live with climate change. The mass die-off of some animal species important for soil development, such as earthworms, was frightening. Without them, the fertile topsoil would degenerate into desert. Hopefully, it was shown that soils established with a diversity of plants rather than a monoculture were considerably more resistant to the changes. Planting diversity will perhaps be a decisive criterion for the survival of agriculture.

Climate change is probably also an important cause of the increasing extinction of species in the animal and plant world. Currently, according to an estimate by the World Biodiversity Council IPBES, of an extrapolated eight million animal and plant species worldwide, one million could be threatened with extinction. In the past, climate change has often caused major waves of species extinction. Today, in addition to climate change, there are other man-made causes of species extinction, such as the application of pesticides, increasing deforestation and islandization of tropical forests, urban sprawl, and the introduction of alien animal and plant species through international traffic. Such additional alien species can severely damage native flora and fauna. A higher priority of nature conservation and generous designation of protected areas would be necessary measures to limit species extinction.

New diseases could spread to areas where they have not been seen before. With further warming, malaria and other tropical diseases with their vectors could also become indigenous to Europe and North America. The first cases of tropical diseases have already occurred in southern Europe. The cultural heritage of mankind is also in danger. Paper documents and cultural monuments such as buildings or museums are also exposed to the effects of climate change. With warming, humidity or flooding, documents, buildings, and landscapes are threatened by accelerated deterioration or even immediate destruction.

Even though it has long been obvious that climate change is not coming someday, but is already here and progressing, the world has so far remained surprisingly unimpressed by it. At best, most people look to politicians and wait for their decisions. But little comes from there; catastrophe announcements and corresponding measures are unpopular, and elections cannot be won with them.

Migration

We imagine a small island somewhere in the middle of the Pacific, a tropical paradise with a population of a few hundred people who have lived there for centuries in harmony with themselves and nature. The island is flat, rising just two meters above sea level at its highest point. The wonderful wide sandy beaches disappear into the sea during the daily small tide and reappear a few hours later. But now there is a problem: the sea level has been rising for years, very slowly, perhaps just one to two centimeters per year. But on this flat island, this is already threatening. First the beautiful coastal road was partially covered with water at high tide, now it is already permanently under water. The small houses directly on the beach, once so popular with the locals as well as with the few tourists, now have permanently wet feet and stand empty. There are no tourists now. The population is retreating more and more to the interior of the island, and space is slowly becoming tight. And then the council of elders decides to abandon the island soon. Contact is made with the administrations of neighboring larger and higher islands, with the question of a gradual resettlement of the population. A fictional story? No, there are already islands in the Pacific in exactly this situation. And not only there, in the Indian Ocean it is the Maldives that will have the same problems in a few years. Because the rise of the sea level is just accelerating. It's not just the islands that are affected either, shallow coastal regions like the Netherlands are also threatened by this sea rise. On the coast of Fairbourne, a village in the north of Wales/UK, the annual rise so far is just under five millimeters. Raising the dike for the few houses would be too expensive, the village is abandoned, and the inhabitants are to be relocated.

A complete melting of the Arctic ice masses over land would cause sea levels to rise by several meters. Low-lying regions might have to give up large parts of their land area, and the Maldives would disappear into the sea. Their people would have to be resettled. The resulting migration, which on the small Pacific island would only amount to the relocation of a manageable group, would assume considerable proportions. In the Netherlands, great efforts are being made to counteract this development. Dams are being raised and endangered land areas are also being elevated.

But this is only one effect of climate change, which is leading to large migrations. Worse effects will perhaps come from the spread of large drought zones. Approaches to this are being observed right now in Germany, even more so in southern Europe, and even more intensively in Africa and across the Atlantic in California. In drought zones, there is a shortage of water, groundwater is also declining, and agriculture is dying. Lack of food resources and water shortages are driving populations out of the region. Those who can still afford it are also traveling long distances to relocate to friendlier regions.

Other regions of the world are currently being hit by increasing weather disasters. There have probably never been as many hurricanes up to the highest category 5 as in 2020. As recently as November 2020, two severe hurricanes destroyed parts of Central America at weekly intervals, and numerous severe typhoons also passed over the Philippines. Not only did the destructive power of the storms, which raged at speeds of up to more than 250 km/h, cause the severe damage, the storms also carried huge amounts of rain, causing major flooding. The water that became scarce in many regions of the world was available in destructive abundance in other regions.

If this trend of drought zones on the one hand and stormy areas on the other continues, then vast regions of the earth will become increasingly uninhabitable. This will trigger migration movements whose dimensions will make the current refugee discussions in Europe look rather insignificant. Managing the coming migration flows properly and, above all, peacefully will require quite different efforts than the sometimes rather petty discussions and quarrels in Europe about taking in a few hundred thousand refugees from current crisis areas. According to the UN Refugee Agency (UNHCR), 80 million people worldwide were fleeing their homes in December 2020, more than ever before, and the trend is upward. However, the UNHCR bases its estimate on a broad definition of "flight," while other estimates realistically put the number of actual refugees at around 15 to 20 million.

What often goes unmentioned in these discussions is the benefit of migration to host countries. On the contrary, the debate often tends to be very emotional, fueled by diffuse fears of job loss, problems of understanding, disorderly conditions, and even increased criminality. Of course, there are also criminal elements among migrants, and these are to be treated according to law and justice. But probably it is rather a selection of more educated people who decide to migrate at an early stage. Leaving one's homeland is a serious and for many people hardly imaginable decision. Is it not therefore the intellectually more agile and flexible, perhaps also richer people, who can more easily and earlier take such a decision and put it into practice? A rich national economy like ours not only tolerates a large number of migrants, but it also virtually needs them. In most cases, migrants are initially willing to take on simple jobs for which locals can hardly be found. And the increasing shortage of skilled workers in Germany's industry and skilled trades, which is already being bemoaned, can only be remedied in the long term if migrants are also trained as skilled workers. The additional demand is in the hundreds of thousands.

To make this benefit tangible, all that is needed is rational migration management, certainly a solvable task. But a lot has gone wrong with this task here, probably due to excessive demands in the unregulated refugee rush of 2015. First, clear immigration rules must be established and enforced. Legal immigration, especially of skilled workers, is desired and can be promoted. Migrants seeking protection, on the other hand, are treated according to the provisions of asylum law or, if necessary, other protection regulations. Then it is a matter of communication, existing prejudices on both sides must be reduced. Even in the chaotic situation of 2015, the basic mood of the population toward refugees in many places was initially one of welcome. Such a welcoming culture should be required and supported by the state. All migrants must be integrated into our culture and way of life as quickly as possible. An offer of integration measures and language courses must be compulsory throughout the country. It will pay off many times after a short time. Housing migrants in camps with a work ban is nonsensical and counterproductive; it promotes ghetto mentality and criminality. Migrants who are well received and supported, who are given job opportunities and see career possibilities, will find a positive relationship with their new homeland and make an important contribution to the national economy. However, it is also clear that there are capacity limits to such effective admission management. Neither the capacity nor the willingness to absorb must be overstretched in the process. Such an "upper limit" on annual migrant intake must be determined by need and actual available capacity, not by political views and arbitrary determinations. Currently, about 28,000 foreign skilled workers came to Germany in 2019, and in 2020, despite Corona, the number was estimated to be several more. Most of the recruited professionals came from the Philippines, Mexico and Brazil and found employment in the healthcare sector. They were actively recruited because the shortage of specialists in German hospitals is now glaring.

If politicians in Germany and around the world fail in jumping over their shadows and establishing sensible migration management, then wars over food, water and land could be the result in the future. No one seriously wants that, but will international politics make that leap?

The Mysterious World of the Oceans

The oceans seem to be infinitely large, but in fact they are also only a limited habitat for their inhabitants. This is increasingly endangered by human influences and already partially overtaxed. Actually, we still know very little about the living creatures in the depths of the oceans and about the processes that take place in them. Undoubtedly, there are also a variety of species in the deep that we have never seen before. Marine research is difficult; at depth there is darkness and high pressure. For humans, these are extremely inhospitable environmental conditions. Similar to meteorology, today relationships and processes are represented in digital models, the accuracy of which is then verified as far as possible by measurements.

The supposed infinity of the oceans has so far led mankind to treat this habitat quite carelessly, its sensitivity was not recognized for a long time. The worst sins of the past and present are the contamination of the water with oil and radioactivity, the littering of the oceans especially with plastic and overfishing.

The most blatant carelessness in dealing with the oceans are probably the numerous nuclear weapons tests under water. Details of these are regularly subject to secrecy, but allegedly some 200 such tests were conducted in the South Pacific between 1966 and 1996. The widespread effects on marine nature were probably catastrophic and permanent. But the discharge of radioactive wastewater since the Fokushima nuclear accident in March 2011 also continues to cause widespread significant pollution of marine nature.

More tangible, on the other hand, is the pollution of water with oil, because oil is lighter than water and therefore initially remains visible on the surface. For humans, oil makes water undrinkable, even in the smallest dilutions of one in a million. Similarly, oil slicks on the sea poison the habitats of marine life over large areas and thus contribute to the extinction of species. In the public eye, the occasional oil spills caused by damaged tankers or defective drilling rigs attract the most attention. People are moved by the sight of oil-smeared beaches or the plumage of seabirds. Largely unnoticed, on the other hand, is the rather more serious regular discharge of oil by commercial shipping, e.g. by cleaning the tanks on the high seas. But global shipping is also one of the biggest environmental offenders in terms of air pollution and CO_2 emissions. It alone accounts for around 2.5 percent of global CO_2 emissions. More modern ships that use liquefied gas instead of heavy fuel oil help to reduce emissions. For future ships, experiments are being conducted with ammonia-based fuel that no longer emits CO_2 when burned.

Garbage is increasingly washing up on beautiful beaches, depending on the current. This brings to everyone's attention a problem that mariners have long reported, the increasing littering of the world's oceans. From packs of chewing gum to fishing nets to fully loaded sea containers, it is estimated that more than 100 million tons of trash now float on and in the oceans. And every day, rivers and wild garbage dumps wash more trash into the sea. This is easier and cheaper than disposing of the garbage on land. In addition, there are about 3 million shipwrecks lying at the bottom of the sea, according to a UNESCO estimate, some of which contain oil, chemicals, or even radioactive substances. The waste not only endangers the ocean habitat, but also shipping. A collision with a fallen sea container can mean sinking for a smaller boat; this topic has even been the subject of a movie.

Plastic waste is particularly critical for the oceans because plastics are very persistent. They do not compost and are very resistant to external influences. They also do not decompose or dissolve in the stomachs of marine life. Scientists estimate that there are 270,000 tons of plastic on the surface of the oceans alone. The material breaks down into smaller and smaller pieces down to microparticles, which then sink to the depths. Fish and other sea creatures regard plastic waste as prey; they ultimately die from larger pieces. They return the microparticles to humans in the flesh of edible fish. The countless "discarded" fishing nets also often become a deadly trap for larger sea creatures. Currently, the Corona crisis further exacerbates the problem with spent face masks and latex gloves. They are necessary for protecting humans from infection but are dangerous and often deadly to marine life when they enter the ocean as waste. An estimated 1.5 billion face masks washed into the oceans in 2020, adding up to about 6,200 tons of additional plastic waste. The polyesters and polypropylenes used for the masks are exceptionally durable.

One small solution could be an increasing use of "bioplastics" (biopolymers). These are plastics that are made entirely or partly from renewable raw materials and are therefore compostable. Certainly, biopolymers cannot cover the broad spectrum of plastic applications. For example, one application would be as plastic bags for transporting food from the market or food waste to composting. Other approaches build on better recycling opportunities for plastics, for example, by using only one substance instead of plastic blends for packaging. Alternatives to conventional plastic applications tend to be more expensive, so a widespread switch would require legislation.

Recently, there have been multiple considerations on how to remove plastic from the oceans again. To collect the plastic from the ocean surface, there are some specially designed vessels from promising pilot projects. One of them, the "Manta," was developed by Swiss circumnavigator Yvan Bourgnon. In view of the daily further influx of waste from rivers and dumps into the oceans, such projects seem like a Sisyphean task. At the very least, further littering of the oceans should first be stopped at each source.

A federal agency for leap innovation, founded in Leipzig in 2019, has set itself the task of identifying and promoting groundbreaking research and development projects. A current project against marine pollution with plastics is also being supported there. The idea is to use tiny air bubbles to filter microplastics out of the water. Nothing should be declared impossible from the outset.

Countless fish and other marine animals live in the oceans, sometimes in huge schools. A seemingly inexhaustible source of food also for humans, which they have also gladly helped themselves to since time immemorial. With increasing demand from growing populations on the continents, and with ever more sophisticated technology, the quantities of fish caught from the world's oceans have also increased. Today, a total of 80 million tons of fish are taken from the oceans every year. This is virtually plundering the limited fish resources of the oceans. Overfishing of the oceans takes place virtually worldwide and is considered the greatest threat to the health of the oceans and the survival of its inhabitants. Overfishing means that more fish are permanently caught in a body of water than grow back or immigrate through natural reproduction. 33 percent of commercial fish stocks worldwide are classified as overfished, 41 percent in the North and Baltic Seas, and as much as 62 percent in the Mediterranean and Black Seas. However, more precise data is lacking for many fish stocks. However, it is not only the number of fish caught that is criticized, but also the fishing methods. Heavy trawl nets destroy the seabed with all its flora and fauna. Numerous fish and marine animals get caught in the nets, which are often too narrow, are not utilized and die.

It is therefore essential to stop overfishing in order not to risk the loss of entire fish species and thus of this food source. In the fishing sector of the European Union (EU), catch quotas, i.e., maximum quantities per year, are set within the framework of the Common Fisheries Policy (CFP). The EU receives scientific advice from the International Council for the Exploration of the Sea (ICES). However, the agreed catch quotas often exceed the scientifically advised quantities. In addition, there is apparently a not inconsiderable proportion of illegal and undocumented fishing, which is estimated at a volume of up to 26 million tons worldwide, i.e., a good quarter of the total catch. The fact that considerable financial interests are at play in the distribution of fishing rights was very clearly demonstrated by the bitter dispute over fishing rights between the EU and the UK in connection with Brexit. Unfortunately, the compromise finally reached was not really aimed at ending overfishing. The dispute also made it clear that the limits on catches also affect the livelihoods of fishing personnel, from individual fishermen in small boats in developing countries to sailors on modern fishing trawlers. This does not make ending overfishing any easier.

The higher concentration of CO_2 in the atmosphere is also making itself felt in the water of the oceans. It causes the pH-level of the water stored in the clouds to drop, the cause of "acid rain." This damages vegetation on land, especially forests are affected. In the ocean habitat, too, numerous creatures and food chains are damaged by increasing acidity. Particularly affected are corals, crustaceans, and shellfish, which can no longer build up their calcareous armor to the usual strength. The warming of the water also plays a role in the corals' degradation processes. The importance of corals can hardly be overestimated. Together with tropical rainforests, warm-water coral reefs represent the habitats with the highest biodiversity on Earth. The infinite beauty of the underwater world, but also of the green-blue lagoons formed by coral reefs with palm-covered beaches, have a paradisiacal attraction for many people. But there is much more to it. For millions of years, coral reefs have bound large amounts of CO_2 from the atmosphere, converted it into calcium carbonate structures and thus rendered it harmless. At the same time, oxygen was produced, without which higher life and thus humans themselves could not have evolved. Now this ecological system is out of balance, the conversion of corals is stagnating or reversing. Likewise, the barrier protection that coral reefs provide to coasts is being lost.

What a solution might look like to the multiple problems threatening our oceans is still largely unclear. The only certainty is that national efforts will not be enough. A solution is only conceivable in the joint creation of rules and action within the framework of an international initiative. The protection of the ocean habitat with its fish stocks as an important source of human food should be worth this joint effort.

Order in Space

Space has a similar litter problem to the oceans. Since Sputnik, the first satellite, was launched into space in 1957, humanity has used satellites and space-flight to leave more than 28,000 objects in Earth orbit, according to current records. Most of them are now debris orbiting the Earth at different altitudes or even in elliptical orbits. Their average speed is around 28,000 km/h. There is no "traffic order" in space. These objects are therefore increasingly becoming a danger to today's satellites and spacecraft. Collisions in space usually end in total loss. With the enormous importance that satellite-based navigation and control now have for many areas of our daily lives, the threat is not only in space, but also affects our lives on Earth.

The first companies, such as Clearspace or Astroscale, have now specialized in collecting space debris again or transporting it back into the Earth's atmosphere to burn up. This is technically possible but is still incomparably more difficult and expensive than collecting trash on the ocean surface. Politically, it is also explosive since the ownership of the flying objects is often unknown and there are also military objects in space.

As is often the case, the problem can only be solved satisfactorily through international cooperation, perhaps starting with a common traffic regime.

Resources in Waste

However, most of the man-made garbage does not go into the oceans and certainly not into space but is deposited on land or incinerated. Garbage is not a worthless material, but contains many important resources that could be recycled, some of which are already in short supply in natural deposits. However, recycling of materials requires that they can be recovered from garbage. This is best done by separating waste before it is deposited. Recyclable materials are sorted out in advance and sent for recycling separately. For some materials, such as glass, paper, and metal, this seems to have worked quite well for some time.

The total amount of garbage is impressive: In the EU alone, it is about 2.6 billion tons per year, with an upward trend, already by about 20 percent since the year 2000. The Corona crisis has accelerated the growth even further, with much more packaging material in the mail order and catering sectors than before the pandemic. Waste separation in Germany is highly praised, but it only works in part. The industry calculates that up to 50 percent of waste is "misdirected," i.e., waste ends up in the wrong garbage can. Hazardous waste such as batteries also ends up in every second household waste garbage can.

An important cause of the waste problem already lies in the functioning principle of our economy. Production volume creates sales and profits. Durable and long-lasting products are not desired, because the decay or obsolescence of the product creates new sales.

The textile industry lives by the annual dictates of fashion. Vast quantities of unsold textiles are destroyed because they are no longer fashionable. For the same reason, clothing is discarded by consumers even though it would still be good to use.

This turnover-driven production and consumption behavior exists in many industries, including telecommunications. The iPhone, like other smartphones, appears annually as a new model, often with only minor relevant improvements. Advertising ensures that a new model is bought after 2 to 3 years at the latest, even though the device would still work well for a few more years. However, the manufacturers do not make longer use easy. The possibility of repairs is limited by design. Software updates are also no longer available for older models after a few years. The same applies to televisions and many other electronic consumer goods. And yet smartphones contain particularly valuable resources such as gold, copper, and rare earths, some of which are already in short supply worldwide. Organized recycling of these devices would be even more important, but at least this is not happening across the board. It is estimated that up to 200 million old smartphones lie around unused somewhere and are not recycled - or end up illegally in household waste.

Important raw materials that are slowly running out due to enormous consumption and lack of recycling are also the building materials sand and gravel. Around 200 metric tons of it are contained in a single-family house. The building rubble produced when a house is demolished or remodeled is hardly ever recycled, and if recycled at all, then only in inferior form, for example as bulk material for road construction. Styrofoam, which is used en masse for the thermal insulation of buildings, usually ends up as hazardous waste in incineration when it is demolished, euphemistically also referred to as "thermal recycling," without any mention of the exhaust gas pollution with harmful substances.

The increasing scarcity - and thus rising cost - of raw materials is making recycling increasingly interesting for the manufacturing industry. In the case of raw materials such as rare earths, recycling will soon be essential to avoid supply bottlenecks due to a shortage of raw materials. But even in the case of bulk materials such as sand and gravel for the construction industry, price increases are now prompting people to think about alternatives and recycling. Overall, German industry currently uses an estimated 15 percent recycled materials for the raw materials it needs, and the trend is rising. In the case of plastics, the figure is still somewhat lower, as the production of new plastics is still cheap. Only rising oil prices or government regulations will make recycling more attractive here. Political discussions in Germany and in the EU-Commission are considering, for example, a tax on crude oil for the production of plastics similar to that on gasoline and diesel. Up to now, plastics producers have been exempted from this. A building materials tax on sand and gravel could accelerate the search for alternative forms of construction. A right to repair or a legally extended warranty period would help extend the life of appliances. A deposit on smartphones could arguably increase recycling rates. Some of these measures are already a reality in other countries. The problem is recognized, and an emerging zero-waste movement opens up good opportunities for creative ideas and corresponding start-ups.

Some economists and political scientists go far beyond the increased use of recycling in their demands, as they believe this would not be enough. They call for abandoning today's growth economy, which means a very fundamental system change that still seems difficult to imagine today. For a long time, national economies have preferably been measured and evaluated by their economic growth. Criticism of this yardstick, however, was voiced as early as 1972 by the Club of Rome in its widely acclaimed bestseller "Limits to Growth," since in its view there could be no unlimited growth on a planet with limited resources. Reality now seems to be catching up with these forecasts, which were still bold at the time.

Time for Change

So, there are some serious problems to solve, first and foremost stopping climate change. To do this, some things must change, that is obvious.

Every individual contributes to the current environmental problems with his or her behavior, his or her way of life. We eat meat and fish, produce waste, especially plastic waste. We use energy for heating and electricity, move our cars, fly to our vacation destinations, and buy products and food that have been transported a long way. Who knows, for example, that most cut roses come from Ecuador? The fruits on the supermarket shelves in winter come from Peru, from Brazil, from Africa or some even from New Zealand? Why is wine transported in large quantities from Australia, New Zealand, South Africa, and Chile to Europe, when here in Europe many of the best vineyards and estates are at home?

But the criticism of this way of life is getting louder, a "re-education" of the citizens is already in full swing. For habits that were previously quite normal, the citizen now hears appeals, admonitions and sometimes even insults from environmental organizations, but increasingly also from his fellow citizens. Only the policy holds itself conspicuously covered; one could make itself unpopular. The citizen's favorite habits are demonized until his desire to fly turns into flight shame, the SUV is hidden in the garage and his Argentinean beef steak gets stuck in his throat. His remaining car trips become torture as lanes are generously converted into "environmental lanes" for buses and bicycles and slow speed zones become rampant. Parking spaces in the city are being made more expensive, converted to bicycle parking, or eliminated altogether. The declared goal is to ban cars from the city as much as possible. Generous, but hardly realizable distance regulations to cyclists criminalize the car driver at practically every city trip. Cyclists are the new kings of the streets by political design. I bought a bicycle.

If everyone contributes to the current environmental problems with their behavior, then they can also contribute to the solution with appropriate behavioral changes. That is the logic of these charges and measures, which many still see as harassment. However, their implementation still raises some questions and doubts. The environmental lanes are just being abolished again in Düsseldorf because a benefit in terms of pollutant emissions is not apparent and is also doubtful. Also, bus drivers were not happy about cyclists on the same environmental lane.

The gradual banishment of cars from the city, celebrated as the new guideline, does not necessarily lead to the announced "livable spaces" in the city center. Conversely, it could also further accelerate the desolation of city centers that is currently being observed. Won't the wealthy consumers needed to maintain the infrastructure, such as stores and restaurants, then perhaps prefer to drive to satellite centers with parking garages? And will these stores and restaurants then also move there in line with business? Alternatively, it would of course be conceivable - against the current trend - to provide the city centers with enough parking garages. This would not necessarily stand in the way of intelligent traffic calming by other means, for example by means of prices or gatekeeper traffic lights. However, such thought experiments are just not desired and are consequently ignored or rejected.

Guiding citizens to behave in an environmentally and climate-conscious manner is certainly sensible and necessary - but it is not sufficient on its own. The individual thoughtful citizen may buy a smaller car, but as long as there are great SUVs on offer, these will also find their buyers. So, the source is rather the car industry with its offers, and thus politics is in a dilemma: It could regulate this, but then it's jobs versus environmental protection.

Even if the public has been persuaded to be ashamed of flying, they will still book the 99-euro flight to Mallorca if it exists. Politicians could regulate this, but they probably shy away from dealing with the tourism industry, which used to be so strong and is currently suffering because of the pandemic. The citizen who forgoes the short-haul flight from Düsseldorf to Hamburg and takes the train, even though it is more expensive and costs him an additional overnight stay, is acting responsibly. But he also knows that this decision will have no effect. The flight will take place without him and will remain on the flight schedule. An effective measure, on the other hand, would be a ban on domestic flights in Germany, or better still in all EU countries. However, not even the Green Party is calling for this in the upcoming federal election campaign.

The fact that the population is slowly becoming more environmentally aware is very welcome. If this leads to many citizens becoming more environmentally aware in their lifestyles, that is good. However, it would be a dangerous illusion to rely primarily on this and to believe that environmental problems could be solved or even significantly alleviated in this way. Both a general environmental awareness and targeted government intervention are needed.

A voluntary "veggie day" proposed a few years ago does little good, since vegetarian diets are on the rise anyway. Meat consumption depends much more on the subsidies and production conditions of agriculture, which are shaped politically. Just as noise can be effectively tackled only at the source, the same is true for other environmental problems. Garbage is effectively reduced by bans on unnecessary packaging and plastic, carbon dioxide by regulations on the energy industry and car production. But increased environmental awareness will then make it easier to accept such regulations. However, the dimension of the problems now to be solved and the measures needed to solve them cannot be handled by individuals or groups, not even individual nations; it requires concerted international interaction.

However, environmental awareness is not equally pronounced everywhere; in the USA, it has even declined significantly in the meantime. The reason for this may lie in the special "American way of life," a way of life in which state regulations with restrictions on freedom are not envisaged. However, an elaborate lobbying effort by the industry concerned and a President Trump who is absolutely intransigent on environmental issues and who has hardly missed an opportunity to deny the scientifically determined causes of climate change have certainly also contributed. In February 2019, Democratic Representative Alexandria Ocasio-Cortez proposed a "Green New Deal" to the U.S. Senate. The idea was modeled on the New Deal initiated by President Roosevelt in 1933, a package of measures to overcome the effects of the Great Depression. Occasio-Cortez urged the Senate to give CO_2 reduction a priority like that given to the moon landing in the 1960s. The proposal was rejected by the Republican majority in Congress, in line with then-incumbent President Trump. Under the new U.S. President Jo Biden, however, there seems to be a positive turnaround on environmental issues.

Humans - Cause, and Solution?

Humans are not the strongest, but probably the most highly developed and most intelligent living beings on earth. If there would be here a higher developed or more intelligent living being than the human being, we would have to know it, would have made probably already sorrowful its acquaintance. Because also the human being uses this superior position to dominate and to use other living beings. Sometimes, when I was attacked by mosquitoes in the jungle of the Amazon region, the question came to my mind, who dominates whom here - but in the end, man with the mosquito spray had the stronger position.

The current problems, plastic waste in the oceans, pollution of the waters, climate change and probably also the pandemics are ultimately all caused by humans. There is now widespread clarity about this - except for a few notorious deniers. So, there is one main problem on this earth and that is us, the humans. For the planet earth and its remaining inhabitants, we are not the crowning of the creation, but rather their largest problem.

The previous undesirable developments are indeed bad, but they could still be controlled, because we are really good at analyzing problems and finding solutions. What mankind has technically researched, developed, and produced so far is grandiose and unique. It enables large parts of the world's population to live a way of life that earlier peoples and cultures could not have imagined even in their wildest dreams. A multitude of developments, from skyscrapers to the iPhone, are masterpieces of creativity, inventiveness, and engineering. Even for almost unsolvable individual problems, such as the rescue of deeply buried miners, our engineers have often found almost miraculous solutions in time. They would undoubtedly also find solutions for our climate problem, for cleaning up the oceans and against the causes of migration. The first approaches to this already exist.

Unfortunately, for reasons that are difficult to understand, this is not enough. It would probably be possible to find and implement such technical solutions in a timely manner - if mankind would not constantly stand in its own way. The inability of people to react to threats that affect the entire species was already recognized by the neurologist and psychiatrist Hoimar von Ditfurth and aptly described as early as 1985 in his bestseller "So let us then plant an apple tree" - groundbreaking for the perception of environmental issues in Germany. For a prerequisite for such certainly extremely complex technical solutions to these problems would be a broad consensus of mankind on these solutions and the joint provision of the necessary intellectual and

41

material resources. At present, however, we are miles away from this. And - even more dramatically - the trend is moving even further away from such a consensus in a completely different direction.

This has a lot to do with a social development that pays homage to egocentricity, to self-expression and self-realization of one's own ideas. The common good - if it was ever in the foreground at all - is becoming increasingly insignificant. Or what is to be thought of it when, for example, in the phase of a new vaccine that is still very scarce, all members of the city council of a major German city first help themselves before the vaccine reaches the prioritized high-risk population groups? Or when one federal state receives additional vaccine in solidarity from the others because of a supposedly special danger situation and then reopens its restaurants the very next week before everyone else? Selfishness begins with the individual, and social media provide an excellent stage for it. The often highly embellished presentation of one's own person and personality seeks recognition in social media such as Facebook or Instagram. The anonymity of the Internet also makes borderline representations and statements possible and promotes a trend toward radicalism. Social media support this trend with their algorithms by preferentially feeding participants information that "fits them," i.e., confirms and supports their portrayals and statements. Solidified groups are formed based on common identification characteristics, which increasingly confirm each other and isolate themselves from the outside world. The big and whole remains thereby outside.

The same egocentric behavior patterns are also exhibited by groups that, for example, want to make their political or religious position or even their sexual orientation the focus of social discussion and elevate it to the status of a norm. The rampant gender discussion and demands for "political correctness" that are extreme to the point of ridiculousness are an expression of the unconditional will of even minorities to assert their ideas and demands in society. In the social sciences, this trend has recently been called "Identity Politics".

And finally, states are also displaying such egocentric behavior patterns; President Donald Trump has put this most clearly in a nutshell with his slogan "America first". Whereby it should be noted that other U.S. presidents and, of course, state leaders of other countries have also followed and continue to follow this maxim unspokenly. Which raises the question of whether and under what circumstances a world policy can be consensual to the necessary degree at all.

The year 2020 has brought this ambivalent position and function of humanity home to us like hardly any other year before:
- A pandemic catastrophe that came upon us in a flash, incomparably faster than the looming climate catastrophe, and just as quickly called into question or suspended fundamental values and procedures of our state for the emergency measures decided upon.
- Human researcher and inventive spirit, who in an unbelievably short time of only one year brought a vaccine against the SarsCov2 virus into use and for this

purpose "simply" developed a completely new vaccination principle, and this in an extremely efficient combination of international competition and cooperation.

In particular, there is also remarkable international cooperation between numerous research institutes worldwide in the development of therapies for Covid disease. The Covid R&D Alliance brings together 20 of the world's most experienced drug discovery experts. Another consortium developing corona therapies is supported by the EU and 11 different pharmaceutical companies.

On the other side, in 2020, was an obviously professionally and characteristically incompetent President of the United States, who trampled on centuries-old values of his nation and humanity, as well as truth, treaties and international relations, who lied, flaunted, slandered, and denied climate change - and was cheered for it by a scant half of his nation for four years. His ignoring of reality and truth was convenient and apparently as contagious as the virus. Many people in the U.S. and then in Europe do not believe in the existence of a viral pandemic and reject the appropriate protective measures. Conspiracy theories made the rounds, even educated people, doctors, teachers and prominent artists fell for them. But the year 2020 brought the election defeat for this president and at the same time the hoped-for effective vaccine against the virus. The weaknesses of mankind but also its ingenuity in solving tasks collided this year as fiercely as ever. Perhaps a ray of light in a just gloomy outlook?

The Failure of Politics

As well as initiative, competence, management, and coordination in Corona vaccine development have been displayed in the field of science, doubts abound as to whether the field of politics would also be capable of such a joint achievement. The handling of the vaccines needed worldwide against the virus in particular shows that this is clearly not the case. The global coordination of the initially scarce resources of vaccine needed for an optimized outcome did not happen. Instead, some rich countries blocked excessively large quotas of the scarce commodity for themselves, under openly demonstrated "we-first" attitudes. Even within the EU, there were breakdowns and distribution disputes. At least, despite the far too scarce EU resources, some other countries outside the EU were also supplied from there. In Germany, too, there was an impressive list of mishaps and failures in the fight against the pandemic: Starting with vaccine ordering, to corruption in the supply of masks, to empty promises in offering rapid tests. There was an unholy mess of decided measures by the federal government and the Conference of State Ministers, which were then either intensified or even ignored at the local and regional level. Schools and daycare centers were closed, reopened, and closed again, at the whim of each state government. Home improvement stores, furniture stores, hairdressers and other stores, playgrounds and churches remained partly open or closed. There was no discernible forward-looking strategy; according to the politicians, they were "driving on sight." The rules were constantly rewritten and then reinterpreted on the ground. The Chancellor, who has the authority to issue political directives enshrined in the Constitution, had obviously lost control of the Federal Republic - and this during the biggest crisis since the Second World War. The democratically elected parliaments also remained astonishingly uninvolved.

In particular, politicians failed to set up functioning logistics for vaccinations according to an agreed sequence. Conflicts among the individual states and with the federal government stood in the way of tight management and organization of what should have been a manageable task. In some cases, valuable vaccine doses had to be discarded.

The order of priority for vaccinations, determined by an ethics council, quickly became wastepaper, and some professional groups and even individual politicians shamelessly pushed their way ahead. An expensive and nearly ineffective "Corona Warning App" will cost about 60 million euros by the end of 2021. It took a rapper, Smudo, to show how a simpler and much cheaper app, Luca, could provide more efficient contact tracing for infected individuals. Together with appropriate use of rapid tests, distance rules, and mandatory masks, access to public life could be preserved, and commerce and business would function again. Despite positive testing, the policy response to Luca was initially very muted. Even after a year of the pandemic, the German government and the prime ministers of the German states could think of nothing else to do but use the sledgehammer of further lockdowns to kill off public life. The enormous economic and social damage associated with this was regretted but accepted as "no alternative". The fact that there have been and still are more intelligent solutions in the meantime is demonstrated by a few regional projects that defied the state dictum and developed their own strategies.

This is thought-provoking, because it confirms the current picture of increasing failures in Germany, which can no longer be reconciled with the former image of an intellectually and technically leading industrial nation. The construction of Berlin Airport (BER) may be a symbol of this. Far more serious, however, are failures and backlogs in digitization, the infrastructure of transport routes and telecommunications, electromobility and, not least, the long-promised reduction of bureaucracy. Long overdue reforms did not and do not take place; "business as usual" was the predominant political slogan of the last decade. Even the bold nuclear phase-out was more of a shock reaction after the Fokushima catastrophe than a vision, given that the operating lives of nuclear power plants had been extended shortly before. Is Germany about to be relegated to the second league? Or have we perhaps already arrived there?

In any case, science has done its homework much faster and more successfully than politics in combating the pandemic. The relationship between science and politics is difficult anyway. In principle, a scientifically underpinned, i.e. rational, policy would be desirable. However, practical politics tends toward the identity politics already described, the pursuit of fixed positions, for example from a party program or a coalition agreement. Science, on the other hand, is open-ended; with a preconceived conviction for a certain outcome, science becomes meaningless. It can then even be abused by interpreting its results in a one-sided way and suppressing contrary results. A policy advocating a particular conviction may not want to argue scientifically at all. Even within the sciences themselves, such a blockade has already taken root to some extent. Israeli historian Gadi Taub sums it up in his essay "When Truth is Forbidden":

"In the last half century, an astonishing upheaval has taken place in science. Entire disciplines have replaced their original purpose - the pursuit of truth - with its opposite, namely a prohibition of truth."

(Quote taken from Cicero 09.2020)

This means that even if the world community could agree on a common scientific consideration and solution of the problems, then it would still not be excluded that identitarian currents would align or interpret such a study unilaterally.

In any case, the world community is still far away from a common scientifically underpinned approach in consensus. This first requires a common institution that is internationally recognized and receives a corresponding mandate from the world community. The necessary resources could be made available through a voluntary commitment by the countries involved. At present, there is no such consensus-based institution; perhaps the United Nations (UN) comes closest.

Here is a mood piece from the 75th birthday of the United Nations (UN) in September 2020:

The ceremony will be celebrated virtually; superbly developed IT makes it possible. But it's just not the same as state leaders meeting in person. U.S. President Donald Trump had cancelled altogether right away; such international bodies were known to be repugnant to him anyway. He had already announced several times that he would cut or cancel U.S. contributions to the UN because he considers the organization to be an inefficient debating society. He is not even that wrong, because in most critical discussions requiring decisions, such as most recently in the Syria war or the Libya crisis, the five veto powers blocked each other so that no decision was reached. For more than ten years, there have been discussions in the UN about reforming this inefficient structure.

Germany's foreign minister, Heiko Maas, sent a message at the UN ceremony: "*No country, no matter how big, can face global challenges alone.*"

A truly wise statement - but likely it went largely unheard. Because no one cares? No one wants to hear the bitter truth that holds the key to solving the challenges? The key, which is simply: Since no one can do it alone, we must tackle it together.

What is the reason for this? What are the obstacles to a common approach? The identity politics of nations, which is always linked to national egoism, probably plays the most important role. If each nation pursues its national interests with priority ("America first"), then a common path is difficult to find, if not blocked-in principle. When a leading world power sets that example, it becomes even more difficult. However, with the highly acute urgency of the current environmental problems, priority must be given to a common solution, otherwise it cannot work.

This is not so difficult to understand intellectually. The only thing that remains incomprehensible is why this necessary rethinking has not already taken place in such a dangerous situation. At this point, the qualifications of the top international political personnel may perhaps also be critically questioned. In view of the widespread inactivity and even the blocking of necessary decisions, there appear to be considerable deficits in the qualifications of many state leaders in terms of intellectuality, strategic ability and, not least, ethics. One does not get the impression that the best of the nations are at the helm here to achieve the best. Whatever else may be the reason for the selection made.

And why is it predominantly old, sometimes very old men who control world affairs, and who are at best countered by super-committed young people? Has a following, politically rather disinterested generation simply slept through the possibility of shaping politics? Where are the younger team-oriented, but also charismatic leaders who have grasped the seriousness of the situation and are taking the others with them to solve the common problems? An all-around view of current world political events is not very encouraging in this regard. Politics has so far largely failed on the issues of climate, oceans, and migration. Can they still manage the turnaround, the necessary course correction? The question is justified, because the necessary unity is often impossible to achieve even for comparatively tiny solutions to problems. For example, the benefits of the twice-yearly time change in Europe have been in doubt for about 25 years. Several studies have outlined that the harm outweighs the benefit. In 2018, EU citizens were polled on the issue, and out of 4.6 million votes cast, 84 percent were in favor of abolishing the time change. Nothing has happened since then, as the necessary unity for a corresponding EU decision could not be achieved.

And yet something is moving on the climate issue, and especially in the EU! The impetus came from Germany's Ursula von der Leyen, President of the European Commission since December 1, 2019. Less than two weeks after taking office, von der Leyen launched a "European green deal" on December 11, 2019, with the goal of making Europe the first climate-neutral continent by 2050. Not only has such momentum not exactly been typical of the EU so far, but surprisingly, the plan also received immediate approval from most EU leaders. Since then, Germany, France and the Netherlands have been striving to take on a pioneering role, and in Italy, Climate Protection 2020 has become a school subject. Now, a good plan alone is no guarantee of success, but it is at least a start. Once it has been laid down in an EU law, all EU countries are then obliged to define the way forward in a national climate plan.

Unfortunately, processes such as the creation of a national climate plan take quite a long time in our democracies. It cannot simply be ordered "from above"; rather, majorities must be won over for important decisions. This is even more difficult when the decisions are unpopular and involve sacrifice or loss. The implementation of necessary demands, e.g. for the reduction of CO_2, also takes time in democratic decision-making processes. But the processes are underway. At the same time, the question is repeatedly raised as to whether our democracies are able to implement the necessary and sometimes drastic changes quickly enough to achieve the climate targets. As early as 2007, the Australian author team Shearman/Smith addressed this question for the first time in their remarkable book "The Climate Change Challenge and the Failure of Democracy".

But even if the EU succeeds in leading the way in climate protection, what are the chances that other continents will follow our example? So far, there is not much to suggest that they will. The path from self-fulfillment to commonality, from national interest to the common struggle to preserve living conditions for all, seems to be a long one.

Another state leader offers hope, the pope. Pope Francis, head of the Vatican State and at the same time of the global Catholic Church, is currently perhaps the only international authority who has understood the need for joint action in solidarity in the current situation and is also able to demand this with admonishing words to the world. This, among other topics, is also the content of his encyclical "Fratelli Tutti" of October 4, 2020. In an earlier encyclical "Laudato Si" of 2015, Pope Francis had already warned against environmental destruction and urged the protection of creation. Now he criticizes in particular "*obstinate, exaggerated, angry* and aggressive nationalisms," "*widespread egoism*" and an "*inability with regard to common action*." Perhaps it is precisely this pope, with his pronounced personal humility, who has the right perspective on events that other state leaders, with their power games, have lost? Even if the Pope's influence on world politics is limited, it is nevertheless very welcome that a globally respected moral authority is here for once putting his finger precisely on the wound that stands in the way of solving our current problems with clear words.

Another spiritual leader, too, sees climate change as the greatest current threat to humanity. In his new book, co-authored with Franz Alt, the Dalai Lama also appeals to the world's population to finally do something about the standstill and ignorance regarding the threat of climate change. "*We humans are the only species that has the power to destroy - or still save - our planet and its climate*," says Tenzin Gyatso, the 14th Dalai Lama, who as spiritual leader of the Buddhist Tibetans is revered worldwide for his commitment to world peace ("The Dalai Lama's Climate Appeal to the World," Benevento Verlag Munich-Salzburg 2020).

The Power from Below

Of course, it also works the other way around. If the leadership cannot bring about solutions, then changes can also be brought about from below, i.e. from the people. It would not be the first time that peoples have taken the helm in the face of inaction or misconduct on the part of those in power and achieved course corrections. This does not always have to be a bloody revolution. It can also be done peacefully, as the German reunification 32 years ago showed.

Such movements from below, specifically focused on environmental protection, have been around for a long time. One of the most prominent is Greenpeace, founded in 1971 in Vancouver, Canada, and operating worldwide.

In the USA, on the other hand, only individual splinter groups acted against climate change for a long time, until the "Sunrise Movement" was founded in New York in April 2017. The concrete trigger for the movement was the policy of President Donald Trump, who persistently denied any environmental and climate problems. The founder, Varshini Prakash, a 25-year-old political scientist from Massachussets at the time, managed to involve the previously most important environmental groups, e.g. 350.org and Sierra Club, in the Sunrise Movement and to share their financial and organizational possibilities. The movement's breakthrough came in November 2018, when they were able to present their demand for a "Green New Deal" to the office of Nancy Pelosi, the leading Democrat and Speaker of the House of Representatives. From then on, the movement, which is essentially youth-driven, was able to gain significant political influence. In May 2019, Sunrise Movement received the US$250,000 Henry A. Wallace Award. By the end of 2020, this now arguably most influential activist network in the US already had 400 autonomous bases in 50 states with a total membership of around 1 million. Admittedly, the new U.S.

President Jo Biden has not identified with the Green New Deal, which Republicans demonize as socialism. But he probably will not be able to avoid incorporating at least some points of the Deal into his program.

Then, in August 2018, a new movement was founded, Fridays for Future (FFF), which aims to prevent or at least disrupt climate change. The founder, Greta Thunberg, born in 2003, started the movement with a school strike every Friday to protest climate change on those days. It quickly became a global social movement, starting from schoolchildren and students. On March 15, 2019, the day of the first globally organized climate strike, a total of about 1.8 million protesters took to the streets, and 1.4 million in Germany alone on Sept. 20, 2019, according to FFF.

Despite the founder's youthful age, the remarkable success of the FFF movement is largely due to her personality and dedication. In just two years, Greta Thunberg has already succeeded in attracting a great deal of attention from the public, as well as from important political and business leaders, with numerous spectacular appearances at authoritative international conferences. Her courageous and clear announcements and reproaches to these target groups gained her respect. Among other things, she spoke at

- The UN climate change conference in Katowice in 2018,
- the World Economic Forum in Davos 2019,
- the EU Economic and Social Committee in 2019,
- the UN Climate Summit in New York in 2019,

- the British Parliament in London 2019, and
- The World Economic Forum in Davos in 2020.

For her initiative and dedication, Greta Thunberg has already received an impressive number of awards and honors, including (at the age of 17) an honorary doctorate from the Belgian University of Mons. Possibly a special characteristic, the Asperger syndrome, to which she openly admits, also enables her for these extraordinary achievements and appearances.

So much for this extremely successful start to the FFF. But now the question arises, how it should go on now. The previous instruments, individual appearances and street demonstrations have recently been considerably hampered by the pandemic and are also wearing out through habituation. They must now at least be supplemented by an expanded strategy. The previous approach in the sense of identity politics, collective indignation over a recognized concern, is not sufficient. It is also dangerous, as it stirs up conflicts instead of solving problems; moreover, a merely one-sided view does not do justice to the complexity of the problems and can thus ultimately even hinder solutions.

The vision has been well received so far, but now we need concrete design proposals and a practicable strategy for their implementation. Science can provide the design proposals, but implementation is not possible without politics. However, the approach to politics is a critical phase for FFF. Joining a party would lead to nowhere if that party is not then elected. FFF must therefore try to establish itself in all parties in such a way that no party or coalition program will be possible without appropriate climate protection. In this question, as well as in the question of the future structure and legal form of the organization, however, the opinion within FFF is by no means uniform. Individual interests and personal ambition also play a role, as they do everywhere. The pandemic has clearly slowed down the movement; under the given restrictions, there have only been isolated demonstrations and actions. The urgency of the climate problem paled in public perception compared to the immediate threat posed by the virus.

Whether ultimately the insight of major world politics or the force from below will tip the balance in favor of the necessary course correction, and whether this will happen in time, can only be speculated at the moment. The ideal situation would perhaps be for the two forces to work together, complementing and reinforcing each other. In today's age structure of society, young people are underrepresented compared to the elderly. A million young demonstrators on the streets then show very clearly that apparently an exceptionally large proportion of young people identify with the demands of the FFF - a clear statement! It would not be the first time that significant social upheavals were initiated by protests of the youth. This scenario does not seem unlikely here either; FFF has successfully provided the necessary initial spark. But everyone must now hurry up.

Freedom

Now, in times of the Corona pandemic, freedom has once again become a major topic of public discussion, at least in democratic countries. Previously taken almost for granted, freedom in most countries has just been restricted in important ways to stop the pandemic from spreading further. The restrictions include, for example, curfews, restrictions on travel, closure of stores and services, and the obligation to wear a face mask. Most of the population has largely accepted these measures, although their actual effectiveness was controversial, at least initially. However, a not insignificant minority did not accept these restrictions on their freedom and went into protest. When radical fringe groups who fundamentally rejected the state also joined the protest, violent clashes ensued, such as a storming of the parliament building in the capital city of Berlin. The reasons for the protest varied. In part, the protesters were probably unable or unwilling to recognize the danger posed by the pandemic; for others, fundamental concerns about restrictions on basic rights were more likely to be the deciding factor. Such restrictions are also possible by decree for important reasons, but they must also be "proportionate". In case of doubt, it is the courts that decide, and they came to quite different assessments of proportionality in the controversial individual cases in the course of 2020. Some measures had to be withdrawn as a result. All in all, despite all the differences of opinion, the picture of a functioning democracy emerged in this difficult year for Germany. The diversity of opinion was also reflected in the political parties, with the Free Democrats

(FDP) traditionally giving particularly high priority to fundamental rights and freedom, while other parties would prefer stricter state regulation.

Regarding the restriction of personal freedoms due to a general situation of danger, the Corona crisis could perhaps be seen in retrospect later on as the testing of the serious case of the climate crisis. For similar measures and discussions will take place in the foreseeable future to deal with the climate crisis. For this, too, previous rights and freedoms will presumably have to be restricted in part to achieve the goals that have been set. For example, in January 2021, on the initiative of the German Environment Minister Swenja Schulze, an installation obligation for solar elements even on private houses was discussed. Freedom of travel, especially for air travel, is also under discussion. But even the necessity of environmental goals is already being disputed by a minority of the population.

Restrictions on personal freedoms do not necessarily have to be imposed by government decrees or bans; they can also be regulated indirectly through the market. If, for example, there were no more domestic flights, or if these became considerably more expensive because of government price interventions, this would have concrete effects on the mobility and travel behavior of the population.

Quite a few authors of critical analyses go far beyond such individual interventions in the personal freedom of citizens in their recommendations and call into question the entire way of life of successful indus-

59

trial societies. Constant economic growth, hitherto regarded as a source of general prosperity, should not be allowed to continue. Their position is that today's consumer society cannot be reconciled with limited resources and necessary environmental protection. The present waste of resources and energy for ever new and ever more consumer products must be stopped.

This means, at least for the western industrial societies, to declare most of the previous ideas, traditions, goals, and values of an individual way of life invalid and to replace them by new ones. This can be easily demanded and well justified with academic arguments - but what about the implementation? People do not change their habits so easily; it takes effort and consumes energy. To achieve a change of lifestyle, important to compelling reasons for it must be recognized, or a catastrophe is already at the door. Voluntarily going to a rehab clinic usually happens only when a significant part of one's life is already in shambles. In a pandemic, a hard lockdown of public life is not really accepted until the ambulances are jammed in front of the clinic and the coffins are stacked in front of the crematorium. Until then, excuses are sought, and exceptions demanded, even by prime ministers who should know better. That's what we learned from the Corona crisis. The crucial question that arises from this is: How tangible and personally tangible for the individual does the looming climate catastrophe have to be on the doorstep to make such restrictions on personal freedoms and changes to previous values acceptable? And will it not then perhaps already be too late, because the climate processes have in the meantime taken on a life of their own?

In fact, sociologists such as Andreas Reckwitz, Humboldt University Berlin, already recognize clear changes in mentality in society, at least in Germany. The earlier joyful and optimistic look ahead that made the remarkable upswing after World War II possible is giving way to a more cautious and skeptical attitude. The unswerving belief in what is feasible and achievable is being replaced by misgivings, doubts, and risk avoidance. Expressing reservations is always easier, more comfortable, and safer than boldly moving forward. Germany is already being ridiculed as a nation of doubters. Progress cannot be achieved in this way. And it's not just the people who are the cause for concern; unfortunately, there are also a large number of politicians and people in government bodies who are obstructing and delaying progress. It is often data protection that stands in the way of important developments in this country, as was recently the case with contact tracing in the Corona pandemic. The cause of this trend of a "new risk awareness" is probably, in addition to simple convenience, the accumulation of crises in the last 10 years: The financial crisis, the refugee crisis, terrorist attacks and the increasingly threatening climate crisis. But there is a direct correlation between an increasing need for security and decreasing freedom: more regulations for more security always come at the expense of individual freedom of choice. Dealing with the climate crisis will also inevitably involve further restrictions on individual freedoms.

The State of Affairs

In the Paris Climate Agreement of December 2015, signed by 175 countries, the Federal Republic of Germany committed itself, among other things, to be climate neutral by 2050, i.e. to emit no more so-called greenhouse gases. This is intended to achieve the goal of not allowing atmospheric warming to exceed a critical limit of plus 2 degrees compared to the level before the start of industrialization. However, quite a few experts, including the Intergovernmental Panel on Climate Change (IPCC) in a 2018 report, doubt that this goal will be achieved, even if - improbably enough - all nations were to implement the agreed measures in full.

Currently, a good 80 percent of the total energy consumed and about 58 percent of the electricity produced in Germany still comes from fossil sources. The main energy consumers - industry, transport, and buildings - have been using fossil fuels for decades. Alternatives have only been seriously discussed since the 1970s. The use of nuclear power, which has been climate-friendly but also dangerous in the meantime, was scaled down again after the reactor accident in Fokushima, Japan, in March 2011, but not by our European neighbors.

The implementation of the Paris resolutions requires drastic measures for a highly industrialized country like Germany. In practical terms, the largest and most essential industries in the country, especially the auto, steel, and chemical industries, will have to be completely reorganized and transformed. The same applies to electricity production, transport and building services. A comprehensive overall strategy for this was not yet apparent in 2020. The only thing that resounds in unison is the concert of demands from all affected industries for state support, which the German government is apparently also prepared to provide to an astonishing extent. In the absence of an overall concept, it is doubtful whether such an approach makes sense and is efficient; in some cases, it even seems counterproductive. An overall concept would have to identify and support feasible and future profitable new structures. Industrial structures that could produce better and more profitably elsewhere would ultimately have to be abandoned here, since otherwise they would presumably be permanently dependent on subsidies. Converting the steel industry, for example, to clean technologies, such as using hydrogen instead of coal, would be awfully expensive in the long term in this country, since not enough hydrogen can be produced here in an environmentally friendly way. This would have to be imported at great expense and effort. At sunny locations, for example in southern Spain, on the other hand, it would be much cheaper and cleaner to produce with solar energy. These are certainly not pleasant decisions for a politician and his position on the popularity scale. So substantial subsidies continue to flow into all kinds of industries and sectors: To the auto industry for electromobility, to the chemical industry for battery production, to heating manufacturers, to the petroleum industry and others for research and testing of green hydrogen technology. The latter, while nice and clean, is unlikely to become profitable here, at least in large-scale industrial use, because of the necessary imports of the basic material. And the aviation industry would also like support for the development and production of synthetic non-fossil fuels. Government aid to business in times of pandemic is helping to let appear such subsidies to business increasingly normal. This cannot be a good development, as it does not provide incentives for economic viability of businesses. Also, the state cannot afford these subsidies in the long run.

Regarding electricity production, the country has set itself a goal: to increase the share of renewable energies from 42 to 65 percent by 2030. That doesn't sound particularly ambitious. But in the power plant sector, there is already the greatest movement, and equally on the part of the state and the industry.

In 2020, the German government passed the Coal Phase-out Act, which aims to close all coal-fired power plants by 2038. This is to be achieved in several stages: By 2022, the share of coal-fired power generation from hard coal and lignite will be reduced to around 15 gigawatts each, then to 8 gigawatts for hard coal and 9 gigawatts for lignite by 2030. In return, power plant operators will receive compensation payments worth billions from the state. These and other subsidies ensure that industry is also happy to play along. Above all, RWE has begun to focus on renewable energies in view of the massive state subsidies. Investments in fossil fuels also no longer seem worthwhile, and corporate structures are being changed accordingly. Conventional business models have been spun off, and RWE and E.on formed a merger for the renewable energy sector.

Even more urgent, however, is the need - following the nuclear and coal phase-out - to promote the expansion of renewable energy sources. However, a coherent concept for this is still lacking; in particular, legal, and bureaucratic hurdles as well as local resistance are hindering the rapid expansion of wind power plants. In addition, there is still a lack of a suitable power grid structure to compensate for regional differences in power generation. Bureaucracy is probably the most difficult obstacle here. EnBW CEO Frank Mastiaux explained in a SPIEGEL interview (No. 48, Nov. 21, 2020) that a normal wind farm today takes about 70 months from planning to completion, compared with 36 months in 2016. He said that up to 200 decision-makers are now involved ex officio in the construction of a single wind farm, and the process fills around 30 Leitz folders with about 18,000 sheets of paper. There are similar problems with the construction of new power lines to improve the grid structure. Thus, the goal can probably not be achieved, already now the development of renewable energies is clearly behind the ambitious goals. To catch up again, some changes must be made to the approval procedures; they would have to be streamlined as a matter of urgency.

On the issue of mobility, Germany 2020 was just beginning to wake up. At the beginning of the year, only 136,000 electric vehicles were registered on our roads; by the end of October 2020, the figure had already risen to 252,000, in each case including hybrids. However,

2020 saw the start of major projects and the formulation of ambitious goals. By 2030, the number of e-cars should rise to 10 million. Volkswagen was the first to launch its Artemis e-project, and the other major manufacturers followed suit after initial hesitation. Whether this upheaval will succeed in this way and whether it will be sufficient remains to be seen. For the time being, the money for this is still being earned with combustion vehicles. But here, too, the state is intervening and promoting the purchase of electric cars with substantial subsidies, up to €9,000 per vehicle at the beginning of 2021. A huge change in jobs in this largest industry will be one of the consequences, not necessarily much less, but other jobs will be created. Other countries like the USA and France are already further ahead. We have a lot of catching up to do and must be careful that Germany's key industry does not fall behind.

In contrast, there is still no sign of any significant change in local and long-distance public transportation. It is currently far too expensive and has far too little capacity to be an attractive alternative to the car. Overcrowded trains and trains with standing room attract no one away from their own steering wheel. There is still a lot of room for improvement for public transport companies. If the state wants to make a difference, it must invest money. There are certainly worse investments.

The least effective of these is the specified target for energy savings. Based on 2008, a reduction of around 20 percent in total energy consumption was to be achieved in 2020; in fact, a reduction of around 10.8

percent was achieved. By 2050, a total of 50 percent savings was to have been achieved. It has since become clear that this target is not realistic. Savings, for example through energy-efficient building renovation or more economical light sources, are more than offset by additional consumption in other areas, such as information technology. With the draft amendment to the Renewable Energy Sources Act (EEG 2021), the German government has abandoned the illusion of energy savings of 50 percent and now even assumes a moderate increase in electricity consumption from 600 to 650 terawatt hours by 2050. Other experts reckon with more like 1,000 terawatt hours by 2050. However, the goal of increasing the share of green electricity to 65 percent by 2030 remains unchanged. Current plans call for an increase in supply capacity of 5 gigawatts for photovoltaics and 1.7 gigawatts for wind power by 2030. However, this will not be enough to reach the target.

To feel comfortable in one's own home, it is essential to have a pleasant room temperature, which for most people here is around 20 degrees Celsius. If it is considerably cooler outside in the winter half-year, heating is used, and in the case of high summer temperatures, cooling is also used to some extent. Both are very energy-intensive. Fossil fuels are still the main source of heating, while electrically powered air conditioning systems are used for cooling. Worldwide, about 37 percent of CO_2 emissions are caused by buildings of all kinds, from villas and high-rise buildings to schools and government offices.

Many climate activists who have recognized the dramatic nature of the climate problem and are calling for solutions argue that, after all, the savings made during the Corona crisis proved what was possible when it came to meeting climate targets. In fact, the lockdown resulted in significant reductions in CO_2 emissions in all affected countries. This was also the case in Germany, which was even given the opportunity to achieve the agreed climate targets for 2020.

However, the price was high. In an astonishingly short time, many companies were financially down and demanded government support. Entire sectors were affected, such as the tourism industry with its hotel and restaurant sectors, travel organizations, and even large companies such as airlines. Medium-sized businesses and the self-employed were also particularly hard hit. Government assistance reached breathtaking levels.

One thing thus became clear: further complete lockdowns, for example in the next waves of rising infection figures, would not be survived by large sections of the working world in Germany without severe and probably permanent damage. The subsequent second lockdown demonstrated the correctness of this assumption, and the third lockdown, which is currently in the offing, will be bitter.

Nevertheless, the pandemic also triggered positive developments. Business trips to meetings were replaced by video conferences. Company bosses realized that this also works and that there is potential for savings. So, perhaps independently of Corona, there will also be fewer conference trips in the future. The same applies to the home office, which experienced a real boom during the lockdown. It may not stay that way to the same extent, but there will certainly be a lot more home office in the future than before the crisis. The saved trips to the workplace alone will generate a notable gain for the environment and the climate. And the employees themselves will be pleased with the time saved each workday.

These are relatively small steps toward the goal of saving the climate. But larger measures are also already being planned or even implemented, as the following examples show.

A Price for CO_2

One effective measure for reducing CO_2 emissions is to put a price on them. This was the subject of intense political debate in 2020, although there was of course resistance from polluters. Experts such as Professor Gerald Haug, ETH Zurich, believe that a price of 50 euros per ton of CO_2 or more will have a steering effect. If the price continues to rise to perhaps 80 or even 100 euros per ton of CO_2, it will accelerate the phase-out of coal-fired power generation because it would then no longer be profitable. The end of coal-fired power plants could then be achievable before 2030. A CO_2 price of 50 euros per ton would also make gasoline more expensive by about 5 cents per liter, it was initially said.

In May 2020, the German government set the price of a ton of CO_2 at 25 euros in the form of a CO_2 tax, effective Jan. 1, 2021. The tax will be levied on any CO_2 emissions and is to be gradually increased to 55 euros per ton by 2025. According to recent calculations, the price of gasoline was to increase by about 7 cents per liter in 2021 compared with 2020, but actual prices at service stations rose by about 15 cents per liter from January 2021. The price of natural gas should increase by a calculated 0.6 cents per kilowatt hour. Sweden has had such a CO_2 tax since 1991, and it is currently much higher at around 115 euros per ton of CO_2.

The CO_2 price has a direct effect on the polluters of the emissions and thus promotes environmentally conscious and climate-friendly behavior. Nevertheless, it is still questionable whether, given the already high tax burden in Germany, this additional levy will cause people to change their behavior.

Energy Consumption of Buildings

The environmental problem of our buildings begins even before they are used, i.e., during construction. The concrete increasingly used for this requires sand and cement. The demand for these raw materials for new buildings is immense worldwide. Sand is now becoming increasingly scarce, so that even beaches are being used for sand extraction. And the mass production of cement generates a lot of CO_2, now more than the entire global air traffic. Intensive research is being carried out into alternative building materials. Particularly interesting are developments from organic materials, i.e., from plants or even from fungal braids, all of which are still at the experimental stage. The use of durable or recycled building materials also improves the CO_2 balance of construction.

The building sector accounts for almost 20 percent of total CO_2 emissions. A first step toward reducing energy consumption in buildings, especially old buildings, is to improve thermal insulation. This would primarily be the replacement of old and leaky windows with new, tight, and better thermally insulated systems, e.g., with multiple glazing. In addition, the thermal insulation of exterior walls can be improved by applying appropriate insulation panels, e.g., Styrofoam. However, both measures are not without problems. Overly hermetic sealing of rooms leads to an unhealthy atmosphere and to water accumulation on the walls, and thus to mold. So, it is necessary to provide regular and sufficient ventilation. Styrofoam cladding, especially on exterior walls, is also a concern, as it significantly increases the risk of fire to the building and occupants due to rapid fire spread.

The choice of heating system is also crucial to improving the energy balance of buildings. Whereas in the past fossil fuels were used almost exclusively for heating, heat pumps are now a much more economical technology for heating buildings. A heat pump works like a refrigerator, only in reverse. Whereas in the refrigerator, heat is extracted inside and given off to the outside air, the heat pump extracts heat from outside and uses it as heating energy for the house. Like the refrigerator, the heat pump requires a suitable transport medium and an electric drive. The heat can be extracted from the outside air or from the ground, both of which are possible during the colder months of the year. If the system works, then the electricity consumption for driving the heat pump is significantly lower than if the electricity is used directly for heating. Ecologically optimal, the heat pump of a building is combined with a photovoltaic system on the roof, which generates part of the required electrical energy.

Retrofitting the heating system of an old building is expensive and is therefore currently subsidized by the state. However, it only makes sense if the thermal insulation of the old building is reasonably sound. This is because a heat pump can only achieve a flow temperature of around 50, or at most 60 degrees. If the heating system requires a flow temperature of more than 60 degrees due to poor thermal insulation, the heat pump alone cannot provide adequate heating. As well as for residential heating, a heat pump can in principle also be used for cooling the rooms. Conventional air conditioning systems work on the same principle.

Even more surprising, then, that only about half of all well-insulated new buildings in this country are equipped with this modern technology. One reason for this is probably the high price of electricity. Nowhere in Europe is electricity as expensive as in Germany because of additional charges such as the Renewable Energy Sources Act (EEG) levy. This probably makes some building owners wonder: High investment and expensive consumption, is it still worth it? In fact, a heat pump heating system is significantly more expensive than a gas heating system - and some cautious homeowners even consider installing one in addition for very cold winters and peak demand. Until gas heaters are perhaps eventually banned - but then there may be no more cold winters here either.

In the regions of the world near the equator, it is not so much heating as cooling of rooms that is needed to create comfortable living and working conditions. There are currently around 1.2 billion air-conditioning systems in buildings worldwide, with a rapidly growing trend, especially in the emerging economies. But not only there, also in the USA 90 percent of all households have air conditioning. This increase is very problematic for the climate, not only because of the rapid rise in electricity consumption. Also, many older air conditioners are no longer leak-proof. Gaseous refrigerants, which have a thousand times greater effect on the climate than CO_2, are constantly escaping through the leaks. Numerous current development projects are aimed at finding other and less harmful refrigerants and reducing the power consumption of air conditioning systems.

The example of wood pellets shows how even well-intentioned measures can go thoroughly wrong because of too one-sided planning. For years, heating with wood pellets was recommended and advertised because wood is, after all, a renewable resource. In theory, the renewable trees could then reabsorb the CO_2 emitted when the pellets were burned. Accordingly, the EU has also classified wood as a renewable energy, and in the new Renewable Energy Sources Act (EEG), wood falls under the term biomass, which should preferably be used to generate electricity. Not considered was that forests are cut down to produce the pellets, which only grow back very slowly. The combustion of wood pellets therefore leads to an increase in the CO_2 content of the atmosphere for a long time and thus to further warming.

Electromobility

I can still remember the time when the most important railroad lines were equipped with overhead lines and gradually the steam locomotives were replaced by the more modern electric locomotives. At that time, I was just at the age where these relations were already understood. As a railroad fan and member of the "Pfiff Club", I observed this development during many visits to the main station with a "platform ticket" for 20 Pfennigs. Today, a steam locomotive can only be found in museums or on a few tourist routes to the delight of visitors. Yet this archaic-seeming technology was highly developed at last, and trains already reached speeds of up to 160 kph. Today, our intercity trains are hardly imaginable without electric drives, and speeds now reach up to 300 km/h.

A similar development is currently taking place in automotive technology. The technology of powering a car by series of fuel explosions in a steel cylinder, which originally also seemed archaic, has undergone constant development to the point of almost unbelievable perfection. Today's diesel engine is a complex high-tech product that hides its explosions behind a quiet whir and delivers maximum power with astonishingly low fuel consumption. Modern filters can (or could) neutralize toxic exhaust gases such as nitrogen oxides (NO_x) and soot particles to a large extent. But there remains an unavoidable emission of carbon dioxide (CO_2) from this form of combustion. This is increasingly becoming a problem because of its effect on the climate. The same applies to the gasoline engine, which is also based on the principle of fuel combustion.

The simplest solution is to replace the gasoline or diesel engine with an electric motor. Compared to today's highly complex and technically very sophisticated internal combustion engines, the electric motor is a fairly simple and practically maintenance-free design. Its decisive advantage is its freedom from exhaust gases, i.e., it emits neither CO_2 nor other pollutants during operation. So far, at first glance, an ideal drive. But of course, it needs electricity. Unlike electric locomotives, which draw their power from an overhead line, this simple solution doesn't work for cars, because they need to be able to move anywhere, not just on fixed routes. Therefore, electric cars must carry batteries from which their motors draw the necessary power.

It may surprise some people to learn that the electric car is not a new invention. Around 1839, Scottish inventor Robert Anderson developed what was probably the first electric car. A three-wheeled electric car was presented as early as 1881 by Gustave Trouvé at a Paris trade fair. It reached its top speed at 12 km/h. It started with four wheels in Germany with the popular "Flocken Elektrowagen". By 1900, about 34,000 electrically powered cars were already driving around the U.S., not with today's sophisticated battery technology, of course. But they already achieved proud ranges of up to 100 km. The replacement of electric cars by gasoline-powered vehicles did not begin until about 1910, the decisive factor being the much greater range and performance of the vehicles and the low price of gasoline at the time.

However, the batteries used are not as environmentally friendly as the electric motor. Their production requires a lot of energy and some rare raw materials such as lithium and cobalt. Studies describe that for each kilowatt-hour (kWh) of storage capacity, about 100 to 180 kWh of electrical energy must be expended to manufacture the batteries. For a high-performance battery with 100 kWh of storage capacity, that is then 10,000 to 18,000 kWh of energy to produce just one battery. Depending on the electricity mix, i.e., the share of fossil sources in power generation, this would typically mean 5 to 15 metric tons of CO_2 emissions per battery produced, and correspondingly less for smaller batteries. Increasing shares of clean power generation, i.e., without fossil fuels, would of course improve this poor environmental balance of battery production accordingly.

Batteries also have a limited lifespan and their disposal as hazardous waste poses problems and requires very costly recycling of raw materials. If damaged, batteries can start almost uncontrollable fires. Disposal specialists are already getting some worry lines at the thought of millions of depleted batteries with all their pollutants and risks.

But there is also movement in the further development of battery technology. Volkswagen and Tesla are cooperating with a Californian startup, QuantumScape, which has developed a completely new type of battery. The so-called solid-state cell is currently being tested in Wolfsburg and - assuming positive results - could go into mass production in just a few years. Expectations for the new technology are high: Ideally, the range of e-cars could double with the same battery size and charging time could be halved, as could the price of the battery. Solid-state batteries are also considered safer because they don't contain liquid, highly flammable substances, so they don't need the heavy casings that cost money and reduce vehicle range.

If the goal of 10 million e-cars by 2030 is to be met, infrastructure will also need to be put in place to regularly recharge that number of batteries. About 39,000 publicly accessible charging stations existed as of March 2021, and by 2030 there would need to be about 1 million charging stations to meet the demand expected then. Fast-charging stations with a charging capacity of 150 kilowatts or more, such as Tesla's "Supercharger," are also needed for transients, not just on highways, although only Tesla vehicles can be charged at these stations. BMW, Mercedes, Ford, and VW also have their own "Ionity" system. The question of who will be responsible for providing the necessary charging stations throughout the country in sufficient numbers remains unresolved. Currently, there is not even a uniform standard for connections and billing.

The switch to electromobility will significantly change the world of work in the automotive industry - an economic policy issue in Germany in particular, where the automotive industry and its suppliers represent a significant part of economic output. Large teams of engineers and technicians, who were previously involved in the further development and production of the complex gasoline and diesel engines and their control systems, will then no longer be needed. The electric motor, on the other hand, is quite simple in design and does not require oil changes or other regular maintenance. Experience with high-performance motors is already available from railroad engineering.

On behalf of and with the support of Volkswagen, the Fraunhofer Institute for Industrial Engineering has studied the effects of an accelerated changeover in the automotive industry from combustion engines to electric motors. The results were more optimistic than expected. According to the study, employee requirements at Volkswagen's German production plants would fall by around 12 percent. That is far less than earlier assumptions, which feared losses of hundreds of thousands of employees. One of the reasons for this optimistic forecast is that Volkswagen intends to include previous external services such as the production of software or batteries in its own value chain in the future. However, this will be at the expense of existing suppliers, who will then have to develop new areas of business.

But these are already emerging, because the switch to electric drive is only one side of the new electromobility. The other side is the integration of essential vehicle controls into the Internet: The car is going online; it is increasingly becoming a computer on wheels. Both developments are already in full swing, the latter driven by the major IT groups from the USA. The control of vehicle functions by a central and online accessible computer in the car instead of numerous individual controls has some major advantages. Adjustments, updates and even some repairs can be carried out online, i.e., without the car having to go to the workshop. At the same time, manufacturers can evaluate important function data from all their vehicles, which can provide valuable information for improvements and optimization.

And finally, cars could also communicate with each other, which could significantly improve traffic flow. This is a small but necessary step for semi-autonomous driving. This is because the car can then give the driver indications of traffic situations in the vicinity or react to them itself. To a more modest extent, today's navigation systems already do this regarding traffic jams. Such information would then become considerably more precise. VW, Daimler, BMW, and the supplier Continental are currently investing billions in such IT projects in order to catch up with the Americans and remain competitive in the future market for cars.

Do we have Enough Electricity?

The coal phase-out can only really work if at the same time the production of alternative energies reaches a volume to compensate for the loss of coal-fired power. Currently, however, fewer and fewer wind turbines are being erected here because many citizens feel bothered by them and are complaining against them. It is hard to deny that wind turbines in the immediate vicinity of residential buildings can be a significant nuisance and potential health hazard due to noise and visual flicker effects. The friendly term wind farm has little in common with the permanently hammering reality of three blades. The shortening of the legal process for appeals that has now been implemented with the Renewable Energy Sources Act (EEG) does not really solve the basic problem. By the end of 2020, there are about 29,000 wind turbines onshore and about 1,500 turbines offshore in Germany. Better progress is being made in the use of solar energy, which also does not inconvenience anyone. At the end of 2020, there will be about 1.9 million photovoltaic systems in Germany, with an upward trend. Because of the quite different yields over the course of the day, however, both systems must exist in equal measure. Photovoltaic systems only supply electricity during the day, most at midday and less in winter anyway. Wind turbines generate electricity all day if there is wind. The electricity production of both systems would still have to grow significantly to achieve the climate targets in Germany.

In this context, the question remains whether our power grid would even be able to supply a large number of electric cars with the necessary energy. The spontaneous phase-out of nuclear energy and the slower phase-out of coal-fired power generation are gradually marginalizing these two low-cost sources of power generation. Under these conditions, it is already a challenge for the power industry to ensure a sufficient power supply for Germany. The development of clean energy sources such as wind power and solar energy is already behind schedule, and renewable energy sources alone will not be able to meet Germany's energy needs in the foreseeable future. Bottlenecks are likely, which will then have to be compensated by fossil power plants that can be switched on at short notice, e.g., gas-fired power plants. And what if there are an additional 10 million electric cars to supply? Electric cars that draw electricity from fossil-fuel power plants have no bottom-line benefit for the environment or the carbon footprint. To facilitate the supply of electricity, the government has been promoting the installation of "smart wallboxes" with up to 11 kilowatts of charging power for private garages since November 2020. These charging stations can be remotely switched off temporarily by electricity providers as needed to cushion power peaks - not necessarily to the delight of users.

Phasing out nuclear power, phasing out coal, phasing in electromobility - does that really all go together? Or has Chancellor Angela Merkel, a physicist, lost sight of the relationships here? Or is she perhaps focusing on future technologies such as space-based solar power (SBSP) or fusion energy? However, these technologies are still as far away as they are incredibly expensive - if they should ever be realized. It would be a grotesque scenario if Germany had to buy electricity from its neighbors, which would be produced by old, partly obsolete nuclear power plants or coal-fired power stations.

Perhaps today's battery-based electromobility is only an interim technology. Quite a few experts are betting on hydrogen as the future energy source for automobiles. For the environment, this could be revolutionary progress. In any case, it is worth giving it some thought.

Hydrogen as an Opportunity?

The element hydrogen (H), a gas (H_2) under normal atmospheric conditions, is available in practically unlimited quantities as a component of water (H_2O). It can be transported through gas pipelines or compressed in containers. In combination with gaseous oxygen (O_2), it produces an explosive mixture, the oxyhydrogen gas (H_2O_2). Hydrogen can be used to produce various fuels, known as e-fuels, which are suitable for replacing existing fossil fuels. For cars, such drives have existed in the test stage for some time. In December 2020, a first Lufthansa long-haul flight took off as a test flight with e-kerosene, which, however, costs many times the price of fossil kerosene.

The German state of North Rhine-Westphalia sees great future opportunities in hydrogen technology and would like to see itself as a platform for start-up companies for industries in this technology. Appropriate funding programs are to support this. The state proudly claims a "Rhenish start-up spirit" (Rheinische Post, 10.10.2020). After all, several founders or co-founders of major new companies such as Zalando, Trivago, Hellofresh, Getyourguide and Freigeist come from this region. For the state of North Rhine-Westphalia, this would be a welcome option for a structural change of its old heavy industry, away from the era of coal and lignite, towards a new era of hydrogen technology. However, gigantic quantities of hydrogen would be needed, especially for clean steel and aluminum production. Minister President Armin Laschet has personally invited the management boards of participating companies such as Thyssenkrupp, Evonik, Eon, RWE and Rheinmetall to a hydrogen summit. There is great mutual interest, and 13 projects have already been outlined in a strategy paper. Thyssenkrupp has already unveiled a blast furnace 2.0 in August 2020, which will no longer be coal-based as was previously the case. It is to be powered initially by natural gas and later by green hydrogen. Thyssenkrupp aims to reduce its CO_2 emissions by 30 percent by 2030 and achieve climate neutrality by 2050. A lot of money will have to be spent on clean energy. The company, which is already in crisis, expects support from the government, not least to safeguard the almost 60,000 jobs in Germany alone.

Hydrogen technology is not easy, however. Cars and even trucks that run on hydrogen have been around for some time, proving their feasibility. However, the whole thing is still at a very experimental level with small quantities and great expectations. The expected main advantage, but at the same time also the main problem, only arises with the use of large quantities of hydrogen, which must be brought to the consumer. This is because hydrogen is not only highly explosive when combined with oxygen in the air, but its production also requires a great deal of energy. To take full advantage of the positive environmental properties of hydrogen combustion, this energy should of course come from clean sources, i.e., using solar and wind energy. However, the expected energy demand in Germany cannot be realized from the given resources of these sources. Green energy sources, i.e., wind power, solar energy, hydropower, and biomass, currently cover about half of the country's electricity needs, at about 2,000 terawatt hours (TWh) per year. Total energy demand, including for heating, car fuels and industry, is much higher again. Surplus green energy for hydrogen production is not available here. Hydrogen would therefore have to be imported, up to 90 percent according to initial calculations. This poses technical and economic problems.

The simplest way to produce hydrogen is through electrolysis. When a direct current is passed through water, the current breaks the water down into its molecular components: Oxygen gas is deposited at the anode (+), and hydrogen gas at the cathode (). To optimize this process, a catalyst is also required, which today is usually the very rare precious metal iridium. However, only about 8 tons of this are mined annually, mainly in South Africa. This is far too little for hydrogen production on an industrial scale. Increasing recycling of iridium is intended to alleviate the resulting shortage, and research is also being conducted into suitable alternative catalysts.

Electricity can be generated from the hydrogen by reversing the process in a so-called fuel cell. There, the hydrogen combines with the oxygen in the air to form water, which produces electricity. And the waste product is water, nothing else. It couldn't be more environmentally friendly.

However, the technical implementation is not as simple as the principal sounds; it requires very special know-how. One of the largest automotive suppliers, Bosch, together with the Swedish company PowerCell, has been specializing in the development and production of these fuel cells for several years. Series production is scheduled to start by 2022. A hydrogen filling station network is also already being planned.

However, the process of hydrogen production and combustion is very energy-intensive. In fact, only about 40 percent of the energy used ultimately reaches the end consumer. The efficiency of today's cars powered by fossil combustion engines, however, is even lower.

When you think of solar power in virtually unlimited quantities, you might first think of desert areas. The idea is not new either. There was already a Desertec project in 2009 with the aim of generating solar energy from sunny North Africa and making it usable for Europe. The plan at the time was to use long power lines to transmit the electricity generated through the Mediterranean Sea directly to Europe. The project, in which German companies were also significantly involved, failed in 2014 due to differences between the companies involved and a lack of political support.

On the regional level, on the other hand, major projects are now being implemented to supply regions with green energy. In southern Morocco, a massive solar park is being built with the support of the German state bank KfW, which will supply 1.3 million people with electricity. Other large-scale projects are being built in Egypt, the United Arab Emirates and Saudi Arabia.

But the Desertec idea is not dead either; it is currently experiencing a renaissance as Desertec 3.0 in the context of the hydrogen debate. This is because the abundance of solar energy in desert areas can also be used to produce hydrogen directly on site by electrolysis from water. The hydrogen produced can be transported more easily and without loss than electricity. However, skepticism about the timely realization of a large pipeline project arises when one considers the progress of the realization of other far smaller pipeline projects such as North Stream II or Bayer's CO-pipeline. In addition, there is the far more difficult question of the political stability of the producing regions and the transport routes. This would have to be ensured in the long term if mobility and industry are dependent on hydrogen, a factor that is hardly calculable from today's perspective. The data security of such a hydrogen infrastructure would also be an important issue in view of increasing cyber-attacks. On the other hand, it somehow worked for oil. However, water is a scarce commodity in desert areas, but is needed in large quantities as a basic material for hydrogen production. Electrolysis of seawater would release chlorine from the sea salt as a byproduct - not a pleasant idea.

Hydrogen as a clean fuel for industry and mobility on a large scale therefore stands or falls with its origin. Converting German industry to hydrogen technology would be perfectly feasible from a technical point of view. However, the amount of green electricity production required for this is gigantic and exceeds all previous standards. The German chemical industry alone calculates that this would require 7 million tons of hydrogen per year, the production of which would require about 600 terawatt hours of green electricity - roughly the entire current annual electricity production in Germany. The alternative option of relocating major industrial energy guzzlers such as steel production straight away to countries where clean energy sources are available cheaply and in large quantities is understandably not popular in this country. The steel and chemical industries are key industries here, and the abandonment of these sites would entail considerable upheaval in the German industrial structure. The state of North Rhine-Westphalia is fighting this development and intends to promote hydrogen technology in the state with considerable funding. It even plans to build a large steelmaking plant in Duisburg by 2025. A bold plan, especially if the plant is to run on green hydrogen.

In the long term, however, the migration of heavy industry will be almost impossible to stop if global warming is to be seriously halted. Industrial locations have always been most profitable where energy and raw materials were available in sufficient quantities and at low cost. It was no different at the beginning of industrialization, when heavy industry set up shop above the coal seams of the Ruhr region. In the future, on the other hand, it may be the wind and sun conditions that determine the attractiveness of an industrial location.

More realistic seems the use of imported green hydrogen in the transport sector. The green electricity generated in this country would then remain mainly for heating homes and, not least, for the rapidly growing electricity needs of information technology.

The Transformation of the Oil Industry

Directly affected by such considerations and plans is the mineral oil industry. Large corporations such as Exxon or Royal Dutch Shell are currently suffering sales and price collapses, the value of Shell shares has almost halved in 2020, and dividends have been cut. The long-term forecast is even gloomier, promising a further continuous decline in sales until no fossil fuel may be sold at all by 2050. The simple truth is that these corporations will have to completely reinvent themselves in the coming years and develop different business models. This is a Herculean task that is currently viewed with great skepticism, and not only by the stock market. Shell, a global company active in 70 countries with sales of around 308 billion euros, is apparently planning to focus on green power in the future. With wind power, solar power, biomass and hydrogen, the company wants to become the world's largest electricity supplier.

One of these conceivable new business models for the mineral oil industry, and at the same time another measure for solving the CO_2 problem, is the injection of surplus CO_2 into underground repositories. What at first glance appears to be an ingeniously simple solution is, however, technically overly complex, and ultimately also risky. To store the CO_2, the gas first must be filtered out of the exhaust gases and then liquefied to reach the final storage facility via a pipeline or transport containers. These processes require a great deal of energy. For example, a power plant would have to produce up to 40 percent more energy to dispose of its self-generated CO_2 in this way. The process is called carbon capture and storage (CCS), and there are about 20 CCS projects in operation worldwide at the end of 2020. A particular risk lies in the durability of the repository. Leaks or even external influences such as earthquakes could cause the gas to escape back into the atmosphere. It is no coincidence that most of these projects are operated by oil and gas companies, including Shell, whose depleted oil and gas fields are particularly suitable as final storage sites for CO_2. Moreover, these companies already have the technical know-how for underground storage facilities. For the time being, however, the money for the investments and company takeovers is still coming from the oil and gas business - a narrow 180-degree turnaround for a "Supertanker Shell"!

Another way to get the CO_2 out of the atmosphere is to use the carbon it contains as a base substance for new products, for foams, sports flooring, or even synthetic fuels. The CO_2 can be extracted directly from industrial emissions or from the atmosphere. The goal is called the "circular economy," a carbon cycle with minimal input from fossil sources.

Travel

In the current Corona pandemic, travel is severely limited for obvious reasons. After all, mass travel is what enabled the rapid global spread of the pandemic in the first place. Two major industries, the cruise and airline industries, have experienced a sudden and unexpected total crash because of the pandemic.

The cruise industry, which has been expanding rapidly, will not easily recover from this crash. In any case, its image is badly tarnished right now because of its massive environmental impact due to archaic propulsion technologies of its boats. Until the corona virus is overcome by regular and widespread vaccination, it is probably only conceivable for stubborn corona deniers to put themselves in a steel cage for weeks in the presence of a globally spread, extremely aggressive and highly contagious virus together with several thousand other people in a very confined space. The industry's current desperate attempts to resume operations will probably come to an end again at the first major disease outbreak on a ship, with all its highly unpleasant consequences for all passengers.

But what will now become of aviation, this once so distinguished and glorious achievement of the modern age? It began just 120 years ago with the short and rather shaky first flights of the Wright brothers and soon changed the world like no other technical invention. Since its beginnings, aviation safety has now reached an almost unbelievable level of perfection, far better than any other means of transport. It has survived the oil price shock just as well as international terrorism. However, low-cost air travel for mass tourism then damaged its image just as much as its contribution to climate change. Formerly regarded more in the luxury sector, it is virtually a symbol of decay that even Lufthansa no longer wants to offer free food and drinks in economy class from March 2021. This is because the former "passengers" have become a kind of human "bulk cargo" over time. This is impressively demonstrated when the airport bus leans to the side to literally dump the people crammed sardine-like inside it in the direction of the plane. Where three buses might have been able to bring passengers to the plane in a reasonably comfortable manner, today two buses must suffice for cost reasons. In addition, "flight shame", a previously unimaginable neologism, was created in relation to the previously so proud industry and its passengers. With the corona virus, passenger flights almost completely ceased abruptly. For months, the skies were practically only filled with cargo planes and private planes. The gradual decline of the industry in recent years thus turned into a sudden crash landing.

Even large and renowned airlines such as Lufthansa are facing bankruptcy or are already amid it, despite government aid. The flagship of the aviation industry, the Airbus A380, the largest passenger aircraft in the world, is being phased out by Lufthansa and most other airlines. The chance of ever being able to fly these expensive giants profitably again seems too small. Whether aviation can recover from this latest knockout, and if so in what form, is currently completely open. The fact that the Corona pandemic was able to spread so quickly worldwide, not least due to air traffic, is only a sarcastic side note to the decline of the aviation industry.

What might the future hold for aviation? Let's speculate a little. Many people have just lost the desire to travel. But it will come back, with appropriate pricing, even in mass tourism. However, we can also observe a rethinking of whether the frequent cheap short trip to neighboring or more distant capitals is really necessary as a weekend activity. In addition, there are anxieties about sitting close together in a crowded airplane, which will not disappear completely as long as there are Covid19 diseases. The business world has also realized that a great many, perhaps even most, business trips can also be replaced by inexpensive online conferences. But whether these joyless online meetings, born out of necessity, will become permanently established on a large scale seems questionable to me. Airline pricing will also play a role. One indicator for further developments could be whether home office work, which is currently widespread due to the pandemic, will hold its own in the future design of the working world. After all, home offices also save time and money, but on the other hand, the problems of working in one's own home environment have also become apparent. Will there be a yearning back to the old office work, despite fuel costs and traffic jams? And then also a longing back to the old business trip with its potential for importance and prestige? Domestic flights, on the other hand, will increasingly be pilloried; they can hardly be justified against the urgent arguments of climate protection in comparison to fast train connections. Either way, even if the number of air trips is currently increasing again significantly, there will still be a long lean period for aviation. Not all airlines will survive, and a market shakeout is imminent. What the consequences will be for future supply and prices remains an exciting question.

With all these critical aspects of long-distance travel, i.e., by plane or ship, the value of travel must also be considered on the other side of the scale. The relaxation, the change from everyday life, experiencing new things and beautiful things, the sociability, these are all important factors for well-being, health and quality of life. And last but not least, flying itself is already a beautiful and impressive experience for many people. The slogan "Only flying is more beautiful" already hit the mark. What's more, before the crisis, airplanes were responsible for only about 2 percent of global CO_2 emissions, and that included a considerable share of cargo flights. Although we are not exactly talking about "peanuts" when it comes to this total amount of CO_2, the harmful effect of flying should not be overestimated either. After all, there are good opportunities for further technical developments in both aircraft and fuels with the aim of reducing emissions. Technical developments have also led to considerable improvements around aircraft noise in recent decades.

I am not in a position to judge the extent to which mass party tourism meets this high standard of travel, but the fact is that there is a high demand and expectation in this sector of tourism as well. I consider travel - and especially long-distance travel to other countries and cultures - to be indispensable for the further development of interested young people. It opens their eyes and horizons, creates understanding and tolerance for other customs and ways of life, and promotes international friendships. These are valuable building blocks for the development into a responsible citizen and for better international understanding.

What's Next?

A happy generation is going to say goodbye, which, at least in Germany, has experienced an extraordinarily long period of peace and has also been able to contribute a great deal to making people's lives longer, healthier, easier, predominantly more prosperous and much more pleasant. However, its essential failure was, in the exuberance of the multitude of positive developments, not to keep an eye on the side effects of this brilliant modernity and to take them sufficiently seriously. Side effects such as CO_2-induced climate change or plastic pollution of the oceans, which were thus able to develop to critical limits and now urgently call for rapid remedial action. A similar blind spot was probably also present in the following generation of today's 40–60-year-olds, who were born into the upswing of modernity and have made themselves comfortable in it. This generation is just about to reach its maximum fullness of power. At the same time, however, from their position of affluence, they have so far shown little political commitment to reform and are therefore probably very poorly prepared for the upcoming discussions and conflicts. This is quite different from the generation of now young adults who, with good reason, are vigorously and vehemently rebelling against developments that will significantly affect their future lives on our planet. Whether the earth will still provide livable or even viable environmental conditions for them and their descendants depends largely on measures that must be taken now by the decision-makers of the world's population.

But how is this to work, with all the political differences, egoisms, and turbulence of the international scene? In my opinion, large world conferences will not bring about a breakthrough. They are very cumbersome and easily suffocated by the diversity of views put forward. It is unlikely that they will produce quick and effective decisions. It seems more promising to me to have a core group of several states, a kind of "elite club," which can implement the necessary measures on their territories as early and successfully as possible and thus set an example as a successful model that can be adopted by other states. The decisive factor here is that not only technical solutions are generated, e.g., for CO_2 reduction, but that solution models are also found for the side effects caused by this, such as unemployment and social changes.

In Germany, for example, the German automotive industry, which grew up on the back of internal combustion engines and employs over 800,000 people, is the country's most important industrial sector and is facing what is probably the biggest structural change of all time - and in the truly short term. The same applies to the oil industry and the steel industry. Not only jobs will change, but rather society as a whole. Not only technical solutions are required, but also new designs for the distribution of work and goods and for the way society lives together. Otherwise, there is a threat of serious conflict in the country.

And this course correction must take place now, at a time when the country and the economy are suffering from considerable after-effects of the Corona pandemic. At the same time, it is recognized that long overdue reforms have been missed in recent years and decades. There is a huge investment backlog in education, healthcare, housing, transport, and digitization - in other words, virtually the entire infrastructure. A persistent demographic imbalance is creating increasing productivity and pension problems. The necessary but awfully expensive structural change in industry for climate protection also comes up against a national budget that is currently heavily over-indebted with an outdated and inefficient tax system. And the necessary serious political decisions have to be coordinated with an EU that is prone to sluggishness, disunity and blockades.

In this situation, strategies for the future are needed that go far beyond the so-called "Realpolitik" of small steps practiced so far. In any case, "business as usual" with existing instruments falls far short of the mark. The much-cited "jolt through Germany" is more necessary than ever, but it can only be a beginning. It is the time for bold visions and the big throw! It remains to be seen whether our country, which is often ingenious but also often bureaucratically uptight, will succeed in making such a leap. In any case, now would be the time to begin an energetic run for this throw. Countries that successfully master such a technical and social challenge can position themselves as pioneers for other countries. It will be exciting to observe which political systems prove particularly successful in this endeavor.

Artificial intelligence (AI) may also be able to play an important role in developing solutions to such extraordinarily complex, interwoven contexts. Similar to weather forecasting, AI can ultimately develop scenarios that are helpful in making decisions about necessary and effective actions by learning to build increasingly accurate models. Artificial intelligence (AI) applications are growing at a breathtaking pace and evolving into many areas of even daily life. For example, there are now increasingly better translation programs into major world languages based on Deep Learning. Undoubtedly, AI would also be suitable and capable of contributing solution approaches to the issues of climate change, cleaning the oceans and regulating migration.

Intelligent techniques combined with market forces would perhaps produce more efficient strategies and solutions than purely political decisions. Although Germany, with its drastic measures of nuclear power and coal phase-out, was the international initiator of an energy turnaround, in the meantime other countries such as Great Britain have shown that at least climate protection can be realized in a more gentle and cost-effective way, i.e., more efficiently. Germany's drastic approach to date has always required further government measures, replacement services and subsidies, instead of using market forces through targeted incentives. Government dirigisme is the most expensive solution for citizens as taxpayers to reach the goal of climate neutrality. However, the solutions emerge, the adoption and implementation of solutions developed in this way will remain a major global political task and probably even the most difficult hurdle.

Fear of the Future?

Dear Earth, we have now reached the end of our consideration of the current situation. It is not a scientific analysis of our own, but was rather essentially inspired by news, publications, and discussions from the year 2020 and the first quarter of 2021. This time was a very special one, decisively marked by the worldwide outbreak of the Corona pandemic with casualties in the millions and deep cuts in the economy and in the everyday lives of populations around the globe. In a sensationally short period of time, however, top scientific achievements produced several vaccines that give rise to hopes of largely defeating the pandemic before the end of 2021.

The summary of our observations regarding climate change is not quite as brilliant. But there is also hope because things are moving in the right direction. Maybe it is not too late to prevent at least the worst scenarios of climate change. Maybe mankind will come to its senses in time, and maybe it will then succeed in bringing about the necessary reduction in CO_2 emissions through a joint effort. Maybe it will even be possible to stop the further plastic pollution of the oceans and start cleaning them up. And maybe an international consensus will be found to control migration so that no more refugees must drown in the sea. That's a lot of "maybes" all at once. Too many?

So, do we all now have to look fearfully to the future? A little concern seems to me to be quite justified. But this does not result from the assumption that there is no solution to our problems. A look at the current Corona crisis makes it clear where the problem might lie. After the discovery of the virus and its potential for infection, almost nothing happened. The virus could spread unchecked almost worldwide. A comparison with the climate crisis is inevitable here. The technical necessities for combating the virus, distance, masks, tests, vaccines, and medicines, were quickly recognized and were also largely available - with regard to the vaccines in an almost unbelievable record time. But instead of now deploying the available means worldwide according to a common optimization strategy, each nation, country, county, and locality preferred to follow its own, mostly selfish, occasionally simply stupid approach. The difficult and often unsuccessful co-ordination of the German states to a common approach is here, so to speak, a small reflection of world events. The insufficient or even completely missing worldwide coordination and optimization will ultimately cause millions of deaths. Looking at this mismanagement, the fear grows that a similarly skewed crisis management for the climate, the oceans and migration would not be sufficient to successfully bring in existing technical possibilities to solve the problems. But there is no need to act so clumsily again; perhaps lessons have been learned from the pandemic after all. I am giving up my own pronounced desire to travel right now, too, thanks to Corona, thanks to climate change, too! But too bad, it was so nice. Any further worsening of the consequences of climate change will now be a painful constant reminder to humanity around the world of the threat, and further increase the pressure for collective action. Therein lies a good bit of hope that soon a pain threshold will be reached that will then force joint action! In any case, it will be a race against time. And the later effective measures are implemented, the more serious and drastic they will have to be. In any case, it will not get any easier.

As an early representative of the "happy generation," I will probably not live long enough to see the result of this race against time. But the following generations will experience it, one way or another. For the long-term preservation of our species, the aforementioned "maybes" - as German politicians are so fond of saying - are "without alternative". Stephen Hawking was a brilliant scientist, and his grim prediction that the earth would become uninhabitable by the end of this century hangs menacingly over the future of humanity. A final maybe is the question of whether humanity will succeed in disproving Hawking in this prediction.

You, dear earth, can follow the happening, however, very calmly. You have survived blazing heat as well as ice ages and collisions with meteorites. Saurians came and disappeared again, just like countless other kinds of living beings. Currently, 150 species are lost every day due to the destruction of forests and the spread of agriculture. Humans, after all, are also such a species. I don't know if you would miss us. But we would miss our life on earth very much. In that respect, with all due respect to Stephen Hawking, I think his prediction that humanity would emigrate to Mars if necessary is wrong. Nobody really wants that. We should rather use our creative and communicative potential intensively to maintain and improve our living conditions on Earth instead of indulging in any space fantasies. So, you, our Earth, don't need to look jealously at Mars at all, it literally can't hold a candle to you. Its offer of livelihood and beauty is extremely limited and in no way attractive. You on the other hand will perhaps adapt your face again and again to the respective climatic conditions, have however probably still a few billion eventful years before you, surely also with living beings on you.

Dear earth, take care!

Thank you!

For numerous suggestions, critical hints
and supplements, which I received from conversations
and messages, I would like to give you
my heartfelt thanks.

My special thanks go to
Brigitte Zakaria, MD,
who has been kindly involved in the
proofreading for this book.